THE
IMMORTAL
DEATH

To order additional copies of this book, contact
Partridge India
000 800 10062 62
orders.india@partridgepublishing.com

www.partridgepublishing.com/india

For parents, now
And Forever

Acknowledgements

I t's been a couple of years now since I had this dream, a dream to turn a random story into a fully fledged novel. And, this conversion involved a cluster of people merging in to make a kid live his fantasy!

Starting up with the acknowledgements; It'll be a sin if I don't start in by thanking the two God's in my life, my parents. I couldn't imagine this piece of book existing without their support and perseverance. I owe each of my cells to them. They were meant to be my parents by some casual fusion while they ended up being my teachers both morally and professionally.

Secondly, to the one who indulged this inception into my nerves and by whom I captured all my will to write, Lord Shiva.

Then, to my publishing agent Antoniet Saints who so allowed this kid to live his dream, also, without whom this story would haven't been printed into papers.

To all my relatives which were my secondary source of information and primary source of criticism. And, to my friends online or offline you guys kept my train on the line.

Then to my teachers who showered their knowledge upon me and made me write with some intellect. Special thanks to my English teachers Vinita Gehlot Ma'am, Anand Sir, Kavita Menon Ma'am, Ruchi Ma'am and to every single teacher who had made me build up my identity which is still far from the word developed.

To my real sister who shares her blood group with me and who has always tried to keep me down to earth. And, not to forget her commendable help by being the first one to read my drafts and edit the initials.

To Microsoft word which corrected my silly faults and didn't let me flaunt, so, in whole thank you Mr. Bill Gates for aiding me with this one, though indirectly.

And, not to forget it's also a pre apology note that if by any means I hurt anyone's feeling or religious sentiments which I haven't but still like a nice little author I would like to deliver my strict apologies to all the readers.

And, finally for the ones who lost their lives in a debacle which occurred in June 2013. They in real terms got in their accounts THE IMMORTAL DEATH.

Prologue

Suppose you are in the middle of nowhere! In the midst of a sacred crisis which would be remembered years after your fall.

No one knew my condition for I was bursting inside, being ignited by the latent remains of my beloveds. Walking and roving around; baring an identity crisis; seeking for eternity and hiding from death!

In the past days or so, I enjoyed every little hour spent with my dear ones, my family. But, then for some catastrophe of a reason I had lost them all, all of them, at one go. Every little creature cited on the previous day had either gone past its breath or had outlived the odds, like me.

A 16 year old boy, the most unfortunate of the lot yet in the names of those few lucky ones! For, in the recent days my trivial little moments had turned into a memory due to the malediction of an unsung presence. My tears had frozen because of the diverse conditions faced by my soul and my identity had disappeared with the passage of course.

Someday you are simply a normal being spending time with your loved ones and on the next day you start trembling due to the gigantic pebbles thrown with a complimentary gesture toward you by none other than the life itself. You would have to walk on fire; A fire which would never leave your senses away, which would induce suicidal thoughts in your veins and which would pressurize you to tie your vocal cords with knots or jump right off the enormously deep valley standing adjacent to you, and staring you all throughout, perhaps inviting you in its inner most heart.

However, the level of Calvary triples when you realize that some night you were WAULKING on the bed of a flower with people right by your side while on the other you had to cross your way from the dead and delusional bodies with no one to provide a spine.

Cracking and threshing their expensive body organs from your own legs knowing they won't feel it but still stabbing them as gently as possible certainly yearning that their souls doesn't get to bare a harm, for a necessity it had become.

Thirst! There was no such thirst we could have ever felt more in our lives, but it wasn't an urge for some liquid rather it was a desire to bring our prosperous and lively days back, it was a thirst for an absolution.

The cracked up surface didn't permit our way in, it wouldn't let us move our leg forth, as for, we were tied by chains made of an extreme substance in the place where we found ourselves begging for help and confused about the situation.

Lovely were those days when we wished to live not sentenced to death on the same front, instantly! The urge for being dead was more wished than being alive and dead, although, it was only granted to some, which so caused our presence there.

There! The place where I lost my family or the place where I lost myself, somewhere, underneath my chest!

I crucified myself for every minor thing including my presence; I wished to exchange places with THEM. 'It would have been better if they were alive in my position and I was in theirs'. I pondered, about the various ways of rescuing them, 'If I hadn't been awake that night I would have passed on too! And, that would have been far better; what if I had redeemed them all by ceasing their sleep? Or for better, I would have sealed the entrance of this place or TRIP!'

I scolded my living emotions for letting them touch this ground, if that would have happened we would have been relaxing on our couch that day, watching our daily program and perhaps being exultant of the fact that we were there with each other or we were there for each other!

But, none of this ever occurred and then I awaited for my death which would take me from there, release all the coffins from my head and thus I would be ending up with my family, somewhere I always wanted to be in and some company that I had always desired for! The holiest of lands became a living hell!

And, I sat in the corner beneath an aged mountain folding my legs and head vertically opposite to each other, suddenly I heard a noise; Suddenly, I sensed my death ....

With no odds to choose I had surrendered myself all ends up; with complete fortitude I expanded my arms to let in the most precious gift of life, DEATH!

For then I closed my eyes to give one last call, however, the memories of the past days where it all began, started rewinding in front of my eyes.

"**N**o matter what you go through never stop believing!"
- Parul Mishra

ACHOO!' The voice came, and suddenly I sneaked into the other room to look slyly for who that poor fellow was! It was end of May and in India you were bound to get sick, especially in the northwestern part of it where at that time of the year LOO and hot weather were at its peak. Last time, when I checked the headlines the temperature was reported as 323 Kelvin. Then, how could haven't anyone catched some sort of influenza? Though, as soon as I looked through my glaring eyes, mainly out casted by the density of the sun rays, I saw my beloved father sneezing around like anything.

'Boy-o!' the voice came from the dining room. 'Did you have your lunch, sweetie?' my mother inquired. I really didn't like those A.K.A names and especially when they were called about in front of everybody, it felt so perverting! Though, I replied, 'Yes mom, I have had it! And, please don't call me that, I am not a neonatal, I am big! I am 16!' 'Yeah absolutely, I won't call you that, KISHMISH' she sarcastically replied.

Anyways, we all lived in a nuclear family, and I being the only child or son to be more specific. Where else, the rest of my family included my Grandparents, uncle and aunt that too a couple of them! Furthermore, I had a couple of brothers and triplet of sisters and I ranked 3rd among them if we go by the aging terms. It takes a lot to adhere the nuclear families, I had tried my level best to combine them but I failed to understand that why we all couldn't collaborate and manage our lives under a same shelter like every other joint family did! But, being an only child in a nuclear family made things worse, the problem of it was that you lived alone, you had to think alone. You had got no one to cheer you up; moreover, you couldn't even confess! It was like living a professional life in the midst of a four walled vacuum contained room, where no one could hear you, you were just served with food, water and oxygen; enough for your physical survival but less than insufficient for your moral growth, and it lead to anti- socialism.

Though, I loved my house and my room, and I wouldn't have given it up for a cause. So, I thought that it was the best if we lived separately, no matter why they called me so self obsessed.

Teenagers talk about relationships and enjoyment, but ironical to that fact I was one of the most boring guy ever not because of the reason that I literally thrived in boredom but it was so as a result of my life or maybe my 'art of living'. At my age, almost every single guy would have gone for a rendezvous with a girl or two, but when it came to my part there was nothing, the counting never began in my case. But, there was always an opening for the odd apart of the fact that I was kind of 'even'. And, so I looked forth, someone expensively time wasting female would enter my door of poverty and ennui. But, things worsen when your own small little brother has got someone fascinating in his life, apart from his parents.

Anyhow, it was almost the middle of summer and it was that much of the most solitary time of the year as it was vacation time and I had no friend to converse with. In, school days I had something to rely upon; but in vacations, all my precious time got wasted with no payback in the terms. Almost, all my friends had turned their routes toward various parts of the world while I was still figuring out my holidays. In addition, MY story was a bit different, we were not economically cool to afford the expenses of an abroad trip, as for, MIDDLE CLASS FAMILY we were. Though, for my part I always kept on persuading my parents, but, still sometimes it made me feel left out. And especially, "When your friend attains some position it feels quite infuriating, some express it as jealousy and some in their part of frustration which indeed is responsible for most of the break ups."

Vacations always began with an expected euphoria while it ended with a sudden dysphoria. All throughout my vacations I used to plan a way to enjoy it, rather than enjoying it. And, I pondered about doing everything, however, ultimately ending up with executing tasks like watching television, or maybe chattering about all day or gaming! Though, I never owned a personal phone for I had decided to purchase it when I would be competent of earning on my own boots! The first piece of my salary would be perceptibly yielded to my parents and the enduring sum would aid me to acquire a phone of my own.

Although, my parents or my little family was thwarted by my recently engaged nature, the problem was that though, I didn't have much to do in my vacations but I still had such materials which kept me far off from my family, and they sort of developed this mindset that I felt superior of myself and out of an inferiority complex towards them I had been unable to confabulate with them, in the past days, or so I THOUGHT.

However, out of the teenage conceptions I had remained stubborn to possibly everyone and initially I thought that there was no remedy for it. But, as I was getting more mature those days, I had to find a way to walk out of it. "And, soon I shall be all over it, back in my normal suit!" were the lines I used to tell myself which kept me from dilapidating my own social life.

2

Basketball is an exerting game, and you can never get enough of it especially when it is your day! 'KACH, KACH' the best voice a basketball player could hear! In sports like basketball even a wise player can tremble in his worst days.

Anyhow, I was playing B.B. and all of a sudden my eyes captured a pictorial representation of the clock which portended the time as quarter past eight. Adrenalin started running all through my blood; I was scared just by the fact that my mother would spread her light on me, thereby, I got furious on myself thus ended up tightening my lace, as I had to cover the distance up by the means of my legs and It would have taken at least an hour or so, with another hour on the clock I could have also imagined a 'Belan' on my head struck with the speed similar to that of 'escape velocity'.

And, so I sprinted along the road managing my way through the TRAFFIC, where at some place I almost died by an inch on the other I surrendered between the road but luckily the driver was not in a mess he pulled the brake of his car in an orthodox manner and complimented me with some words which I never cared about, as for, I got a new life on this planet!

Shaking and shivering I reached by my place, where some discussion was going on. And, I cursed myself for over thinking as it almost took my soul away from my body, and I happened to ponder about giving that car owner a good reply, but regretting had always been a symptom of 'the weak'. So, I carried my regretting attitude towards the discussion table which had kept me from enjoying my day. And, there I heard a debate going on between my family members. This reunion appeared quite unfamiliar to my senses, as long as I could remember this group meeting had never taken place in the previous years. THEY hardly stopped by to even a say a 'Hello'. So, It could have been rather a result of my succeeding persuasion to go for a family outing, as it was all around my head and it was not novel to them. I always kept on insisting them something or the other but they never got influenced at all, rather they scolded me for being such a demanding kid; 'So how come this sudden burst of change, automatically?' I enquired to myself.

But, I was never sure of this fact; they could have talked about something else too, perhaps something crucial, until I was sitting in a bed which was adjacent to the ROOM

OF DISCUSSION and I heard them talking about, 'taking holidays'; actually, my parents in fact my entire family were employed in the government jobs and they only had a limited amount of days in which they could have relaxed upon. Even in holidays, they had to work in their respective offices, "Life was tough for them", and so was for everyone.

Though, I wanted to hear some more of their conversation but then my 'dinner dominating' grandmother called me up and I had to leave the room then and there. Grandmothers always are quite productive about food grains, if you ask for 2 they shall give you three, they called it the 'n+1' formulae, where 'n' was the number of food article. And, for instance if you somehow refused to accept their decision they would start the comparison, which usually began with the sarcastic comments on your figure then came the contrasting part either done against your own relative or the known people.

But, those two words (Taking holidays) had cleared my conception about going on a trip, as it fitted the best in that situation, thereby explaining it all! However, the questions of the hour were- where? How? When?

For the first one, perhaps some costal region or a sea side region would have done as one would have lucidly got his picture clicked which would have set in for a perfect background.

Coming to the second one, I always pictured myself travelling through the air route along the windy atmosphere while conversing with the birds flying outside our window, and getting a feeling of the most superior 'being' in this globe with respect to the elevation.

And, for the last part, I could have gone probably at anytime of the month, or year to be more precise. I had no problem in this matter, whatsoever!

The entire night, I changed sides like a 'new born', bouncing and propelling around my axis, for excited I was to confirm my diagnosed belief!

3

As soon as my eyes opened due to the sharp and glaring rays of the sun refracted by my polished window; quite swiftly I got down the stairs to inquire the previous night's dilemma. But, my misfortune had struck the 12th hour of the noon and my indolent nature proved out to be a bane for me, as my parents had already departed for their respectable offices some time back, leaving me alone with all my doubts and queries. Although, I was lazy yet I was determined to attain the 'known' spectrum of life, which was filling my brain up with cognizance of the near future. Thereby, I decided to get my answers in the forthcoming evening. Once again, my excitement nerve came up, but this time for the sake of controlling the odds I decided to get laid alone, again. As it was the best way to keep my thoughts from intermingling.

I kept myself up the entire afternoon, just as I could cook the best of my noodles. Later, I did my routine tasks and soon my friends showed up. We played for hours and that little daily routine made me outlook the in force task, thereby, we played for a couple of hours but all of a sudden I heard someone murmuring about a trip to New York. It stretched open my eyes, and my dear ear drums simultaneously got a beat to catch, as it went upright. The first thing I did was to throw the ball away and run toward my place, but while running, various thoughts were crossing my mind one of the major was, 'What if they were talking about something else? All my hopes would shatter into the gutter and ultimately I would end up being depressed and obsessed with my life. That, then I wouldn't tolerate!'

With great pace comes a lot of strain! And, I had forever exposed myself to the later one; with those tired pair of legs I knocked my door repeatedly. The interior scenario was quite ordinary; things were on their respectable places with my parents discussing something with each other. Therefore, I had to leave as I wanted to give them some privacy, but I could have only resisted myself until dinner.

Everyone had consumed their grains then and I was all set to ask the "question of the vacations", but all of a sudden a vibration was sensed and soon it began to increase. And, my eyes caught a technological gadget which helped us to create a communicational interface between two or more users. Yes, It was my father's cell phone. He picked up his phone randomly as if some stranger was on the other line, but little did I know that it would take him a long time to get settled. I was disheartened and annoyed, however, I resisted myself for a couple of moments, yes indeed a couple of them!

'Will you listen to me for a second?' I shouted, my patience was continuously mocked and it had to burst within some moment or the other. My mother came running (literally jogging) inside the room after she heard my voice, her confusing expressions could have easily be identified. Whereby, my father stared at me with his eyes wide opened for a couple of minutes with his cell phone still in his hands. And, it had made me reticent; I had no choice but to linger for some more time, up until he had kept his phone down.

At last, after 28 minutes and 32 seconds of long waiting and chattering he kept his mobile down and it opened an opportunity for me. But, they say that only a dog has its day, not the humans.

The clock ticked 9 o' clock, it was my mother's hour to watch her daily soap and to my misfortune it was some special episode of an hour in which the face of a groom was going to be revealed!

She was all set to waste her time, "Wait! Before you start this bunkum, I require my answer." I interrupted while standing in front of the technologically dilapidating box. "About, what?" my mom asked. "What were you people discussing the previous day?" I enquired. "OH! That." My mom replied and had her moment of relief. "Are we going on some sort of trip?" I asked while staring at her so that I could have persuaded her for it if they hadn't made such plans. 'Look, we were just about to tell you' she spoke regrettably, 'Tell me what?' I interrupted, with my impatient reactions. 'That we are planning to go on a trip' she composedly replied. It was a rhetorical reply; therefore, I was perplexed at that particular moment, as my assumptions were correct, I was quite convinced by my performance.

But, I wanted to prove my diagnosis further right, so I asked, 'What? Where? How? And Why!' she was kind of deceived by the amount of questions asked at a go. 'Look, it is just an oral plan and we aren't sure that it would have its proper implementation or not.' She continued, 'So, we are just making up our mind to visit the holy city of "Haridwar", for a couple of days to attend a family function. And, we might come back on the next Friday or so. Though, it is just a rough blueprint but let's see!' she concluded. It was a shock for me, not that I didn't like Haridwar or something and actually I have been into the city and it had a beauty of its own, but precisely my fantasy was shattered. The dreams of sea side or a famous landmark with my theories got deposited in the holy 'Ganges' as the bottom sediments of the river!

However, it was better to be one legged than to be a full handicapped, so I agreed, I had no alternative! 'Ah! Sweetie, I think or presumably we think that it will be better for you to stay here, it is just a short visit and we all our known to the 'immunity level' that you share. And, the trip won't be that fascinating.' My mom replied while refusing my confirmation. A sense of betrayal could have been easily sensed in the room, my entire family was going to leave me in solitude with my dormant grandmother. Without asking any further queries I left the room in a hasty manner. Perhaps, the most commonly adapted strategy by a major population of the teenagers. That day was horrible, but things were just going to get worse!

Next morning, I woke up a bit early and I found my parents standing right next to me, their words were, 'Pack it up!' I had this demented sensation by which I was quite elated internally but I knew how to get it managed externally. The fire that was lit up by the affront last night was not extinguished yet! Thereby, I refused their proposal on the first place. But, my internal exhilaration was more dominating than my external firmness. I had to go somewhere, since it would have given me some material to have a piece in my friend circle. So, I shook their hand with mine, confirming my departure with them, although 8 hours later. Quite a scandal!

By the means of these past happenings I had cleared up one concept in my mind that, 'I won't waste these vacations by jerking off!' However, if my friends were given this opportunity to visit some religious city none of them would have raised their hands up. But, for me, it was a deal which I could not refuse!

4

It were several days then since I consented to appear in a city of UK, that was, Uttarakhand. And, all those days, I was relevantly holding my breath for this one. The Packing Day! After an extended span of time, we got an opportunity to pack. And, in the previous two days, I was pondering about the stuff that I would carry with me. Some would consider it a girlie thought but I had no control on myself!

So, initially I started with folding up my clothes, brush, and some novels. Also, I kept some pre-quested money in my pocket, just in case, and astonishingly, 'I would be trying on various dishes if my father discards to purchase them' I planned. With some extra efforts, I took a pair of earplugs of my father's phone so that I could revitalize myself in unpleasant times. Where else, my parents took their habitual stuff; in addition, they clutched the normal meds, which would have just helped us in the unhealthy times.

Furthermore, I took a couple of bubble gums. There goes a short tale about it truthfully as short as a fact but just a bit elongated. I was travelling in a bus from my native place to a nearby town, and due to the sick atmosphere of the bus I started vomiting which was followed up by a stomach ache and high fever, that strong and pungent essence of sweaty old man sitting adjacent to me made it worse. From that day forth I kept my faith in bubble gums as they facilitated me to avoid queasiness and the rest of its consequences.

I was almost packed up, so I went to my father's room to check onto their preparation, but all of a sudden I recalled a question, 'By which means are we travelling?' I looked at my father curiously while asking that one up. 'BUS!' he replied. The floor beneath me started moving away somewhere; only a bus was left to thrash my dreams up into the trash bin. 'We can't cover such a long passage by bus!' I exclaimed with an opposing demeanor. 'We can! And we are.' He concluded. Thirteen long hours in a bus? With only three bubble gums in my pocket. That was not at all digestible, further I came to know that we were taking a sleeper bus for our departure, but no A.C., my mother did not like the freezing atmosphere created by such instruments, they hitched her. And, she required her bit of rest in at least one phase of the day.

Though, all this was just a symptom of the series of incidents that were going to happen, or so I thought. And, I wasn't sure about the fact that the rest of our trip will be a success or not, and I knew that it would be deadly boring, we would reach in, attend our function and we would come back. With, no memories to recount upon!

5

I ardently glanced at the outer phase of my house with my head held in vertically perpendicular position making an angle of elevation with the sun. 'Kid, call the taxi!' a voice came from my back, 'I am all set dad! Let's leave' I spoke with my own deliberate tone, thus pretending to ignore his words. 'If you are all set then call the taxi' my father yelled. 'On my way!' I spoke with a surrendering voice.

There was a huge haste in my house, everybody was grasping their materials on the last moment and preparing to wave a hand toward the ones who were going to stay; thus, thriving their life with uttermost freedom. Meanwhile, I was serving up on my orders — bringing up the taxi, calling my aunt inside my house for the last moment preparation, scolding my cousin sibling which was actually some task that perhaps every elder brother or sister enjoyed!

I went to the taxi driver but he was rather pre occupied at that moment, so I asked him to come over by our place. And, as soon as I arrived at my place I found my father blaming me for overusing his 'communicational device'. For, the battery of that gadget was rather negligible and he had to switch his phone off for that matter, accordingly he accused me of using it at that hour when we were about to leave. Those were one of those silly depreciable instances, which I had been exposed to, for, quite some time. With that he also forgot to keep his charger in the bag pack.

Just after that little bit of disregard of my image thus impugning our farewell, I had my stomach moving. I was about to occupy my seat in the taxi but then I felt some bubbles rotating about their mean positions in my stomach; the pressure difference was slightly rising inch by inch and I came to know the desire of my tummy when I had almost liberated a nuclear bomb! I rushed to the nearest washroom that I could have found, which was three floors away. Those moments are the sturdiest of all, only few can resist such vital pressure. Such people literally deserve the title of, 'Iron stomach'. And, I could too, fortunately! However, the moments afterwards were rather splendid and alleviating, one could have never got enough of it!

I could hear some voice coming downstairs, but I cared to ignore it initially as I wasn't sure about the person who was mentioned in that voice. Until, I heard my father's voice echoing all over the place, 'This boy is frivolous (ridiculous)! I had yelled at him a couple of hours ago to clear his system out, but at that time, he was just nodding his neck.

And now, at peak of the hour, when the taxi is about to reach in he has decided to evacuate his bowels, let him stay here now!' my ears stood right up, I wanted to get out from that place, but, then it is difficult to do so when you have worked your way in! Satisfaction counts right up the corner, and I needed to be satisfied. So, I made my mind up to stay on the hot seat until I hit the right spot!

Soon, my parents got busy in resolving some kind of issue with our neighbors while I was still proceeding with my relief therapy up until I heard another voice, it sounded as a taxi horn but I didn't concentrate on it initially, although as the voice deepened, I got my pulse back thinking that it was ours! I stood up quickly grasped and gathered everything I could at one go and left the place in a thunder. Afterwards, I came out of the room and hurried down the balcony to seek the confirmation of my dilemma.

To my surprise, it was a random car that wanted to enter our narrow lane! It was a fault really; "Fault in my stars" as some astronomers would call it. I regretted my haste, and I wanted to go back again but it would not have been the same feeling then, so I picked the other way out, the stairs!

I walked down the stairs quite deliberately and then to the fridge to take a last sip of water, in my house! Further, I started touring my house for the last time before my arrival; I began with the dining room followed by our living and my study room. Then, I turned my way toward the kitchen where I saw some snacks lying in front of my eyes waiting to be ravished but I chose not to eat them, rather I made up my mind to attack on them after my return back. Finally, I turned my front towards the clock which denoted our time of departure, thereby I walked outwards carefully locking the entrance gate.

Outside my house I saw my father assigning some work to my grandmother, certainly the daily routine work and maintenance were the topics being discussed. Just after that, he called some of his "official friends" up to let them know about the amount of holidays he was going to take. And, on the previous night even my mother made such a call!

As the clock was taking its turn I was getting impatient again, for my uncle and aunt were still in their shelter for some reason and I didn't find it appropriate to complain or yell about their moderate body design, while, we were standing in the heat burning ourselves under the weight of our luggage!

Peep-Peep, buzzed a voice ridiculously forcing us to twist back, as we turned our heads to assure our suspicion, a black colored, pitiably maintained and superficially ventilated three-wheeler was waiting for us down the road. The limit of our excitement was on its epitome, a speed booster got installed in each one of us and I rushed towards my little palace to pick the remaining suitcases up one last time as I glanced at one of the magnificent architectural representation ever seen by me, my house!

As soon as I turned my neck, I saw my family biding a farewell to my grandmother and neighbors, my father waved at me, thus calling me to bid my bit. I ran in a dignified manner and saw people touching my grandmother's feet, I knew what my next task was!

Once again, I could rely upon my assumption, he did ask me touch her feet, there was a good quality of crowd standing around her pushing and pulling continuously. And, as I bent down to seek her blessing for the rest of our journey she kept a hand on my back, which further moved up to my head. It was a minting experience, one which was worth to a quarter of a billion dollars. For, I was just able to touch a quarter of them!

It felt great and for the first time I had this feeling that everything would be just fine but the question was WILL IT BE SO?

As quick as I accomplished my task my father ordered to me to keep our entire luggage in the back trunk of the taxi. With all due respect and sentiments I followed his order and sat in the taxi, thus, being the first one to do so. My family was proceeding as moderately as possible, eyes wet and full of hope, hope for the betterment of our lives, hope for the safety of our future and journey at small.

My aunts and mother had their course of shedding tears as they sat in the taxi like if they were leaving permanently! Thus, giving a suitable example of a typical Indian woman but still it instilled some sentiments in our hearts. Finally, when all the LEAVING RITUALS were finished with a deliberate manner everyone sat in the taxi, the ladies first followed by the gents and the children. Everyone adjusted themselves to sit in UNCOMFORTABLY!

The taxi driver pulled the liver with a good amount of force, although, unfortunately it never started; one of us had to go and exert some thrust from the back, and again to my misfortune it was me! After, certain efforts we (the taxi driver and I) were able to ignite the engine. I swiftly took my place to sit in an uncomfortable silence.

Our taxi driver was about to move ahead but all of a sudden I turned my back to gaze at people who were gesturing us a good bye, which was lead by my grandmother. She had tears in her eyes and solitude in her mind. We had decided to take her with us initially but then there would have been no one to take care of our house. Furthermore, not a single being was ready to give up his place in exchange of my grandmother; hence we had to let her stay.

The taxi took onto the road with great funds to choose and a lot less to loose, at last I looked at the path of our local place ONE LAST TIME before our little trip!

6

The taxi at last halted on its final destination, and we were all set to leave the city, as we had then already taken out our luggage from the trunks and had paid the driver for his unsafe and reluctant driving. Coming to the bus, we had booked a NON-A.C. sleeper bus with 4 cabinets and 2 seats just for sitting purpose. As I went through the sitting plan I came to know the arrangements in which we were going to land our lower surface, the last four cabinets and the two seats in front of them were allotted to us. And, I was consentingly waiting for the bus, so that I could have rated my comfort level for the next 13 hours.

The clock had then reached to quarter past 9 while the time allotted to us was 9 o' clock. All we could do and the only thing we did was to kill time. The journey was quite a long one, hence the night travelling. We didn't want to be unfit medically cause of the hot weather and winds around the country's capital, as we were going to cross our way from there and also Haridwar itself was quite nasty in the afternoon. Thereby, it was better to travel during night and sleeping than waking up all day and suffocating till death!

All the shops were closing down; their iron sheets had touched the ground. The sky was getting ominous bit by bit, we thought of it as a lunar eclipse but we were contradicted by the moon rotating in front of our eyes. Most of us got tired standing but only some of us got the lucky opportunity to sit on the edge of our luggage. In addition, this was the worst waiting ever, though I remember I waited a lot for a call from my girl-friend and as I never had one, therefore it was the worst waiting ever!

Two hours! Almost two hours got past after my excitement and goose bumps for a short family trip. My impatient monster living inside my skin was about to get unleashed. But, then I saw a blue colored, whitely patched and tidy looking bus in front of my eyes while the rest of them were looking the opposite side. 'Is that the one?' I asked pointing towards the vehicle. 'No, it is not!' a voice echoed from the back interpreting the wrong one. 'No, not that! I meant the one whose tire looks a bit punctured.' said I. 'Oh! The boy is right, it is our BUS!' My uncle agreed with a confirming tone as he continued. 'Grab up your bags, and tighten up your socks! We are going to………' 'To Haridwar!' my brother offered thus taking all the fun out of it.

We crossed the lane vigilantly and stepped onto the bus, 'Is it the bus going to Haridwar?' my father asked the driver and the fellow passengers sitting adjacent to him. 'Yes, indeed!' the conductor replied. Soon, we got in and started looking for our seats since it wasn't that hardcore. As quick as we found our seats we started keeping our bags on it. While, I wanted to pre reserve my seat; so, I got on top of my sleeping cabinet which was as long as my height, but as thick as my waist, later I regretted my lightening decision. Just for the sake of adding to my misfortune and the deficit amount of space my father came up to me, for sleeping purpose.

As I laid my body down I divulged the real height of the cabinet which was rather shorter than mine, since I hit my head cause of straightening my legs, it was a proud moment for me as my mates have never appreciated my length! For a moment, I thought that I got tall but soon the pitiful feeling dominated the former.

Under the stars I laid my head down, a good slumber was nowhere near the corner. I had to change my positions constantly; my fate never blessed me with a good night sleep rather I exerted myself all throughout the night. I tried to make a hole in the wall which was resisting me to spread my legs properly by kicking it which nearly proved out to be terminal!

The night was elongated onto the verge of vexation; it explained the 'theory of relativity' with a properly managed real life example. The literal obstacle was not the night phase rather it was the afternoon session where my visage would be subjected to hot and dry winds repeatedly; I feared that I might get sunburn and the harmful UV rays wouldn't adore my face too. Although, I retreated my thought because we Indians were known to such weather and also we were like really, Tan.

It was around 3 o' clock then, and prior to that I had almost scratched my artery out a couple of times due to those BLOOD SUCKING organisms. I didn't know how to get on with it and the entire mosquito repellant was either with our neighboring cabinet or it was kept back at my residence. I had no way out! "The constellation was my will and I shall fathom it till the Milky Way!" I said to myself, every time I lost the hope of getting rid of those mosquitoes.

Slowly and steadily my eyes were falling from its place, as if I was drugged. Perhaps by the alluring night and its co-mates (the moon and the stars) or it was just a result of the hardworking day followed by its consequence 'the dizziness'. It had something deep in it but I had no control over my nerves, as if I was floating in a lake or I was flying in the sky in my own dreamy world for then the sub conscious mind had dominated over the normal! A state where the minds pull the strings, where the fearsome and affectionate conditions aren't discriminated, a state where you are the ONLY world!

7

I unimpeded my eyelets and I could easily felt the thirst in my throat increasing with the course of seconds. It was about six o' clock in the morning and we were still speeding at a moderate pace. I looked for some source where I could have got my diencephalon satisfied, tough, I couldn't; hence, I had to slide by the stairs to find it. Where, I also couldn't find my slippers which were right around the corner, but then I had to drag my feet all throughout that rough and woody floor. I reached onto the back of the conductor which was purely asleep; so I had to change the direction of my feet to the driver, fortunately he was alive and working, some neck jerks were there but then they were tolerable. 'Where would this bus stop?' I inquired.

He was chewing a poor quality tobacco in his mouth which looked as if he had stuffed some fillings up in it which obviously he did! He gently spitted the tobacco out of the window which stuck onto the face of a passenger sitting behind and near the window. After, spitting he turned his neck towards me and murmured few words in the local language which I hardly understood and that tobacco chewer made it worse! I could read his gestures which clearly indicated that then was not a good time to talk since he wanted to focus on his driving. So, accepting his undermined and unconfirmed gestures, I turned to retreat backwards near my cabinet. 'He says that the bus will stop in five.' The man sitting under a black blanket spoke immediately, for then the conductor he was. 'But, what do you want kid?' he asked. 'I require some water.' I answered with some desirable expressions which were capable enough to persuade them and sympathize a few drops toward me, which ultimately ended with me holding a bottle full of life!

Tough, on the first place I was reluctant to take even a sip of it as I reckoned that they would dismantle me, thus I'd end up being high jacked. However, I chose to believe in humanity, reason why I took a sip from it and waited for the reaction, and my trust in humanity was restored when there was no such reaction, if we rule out the burping! Still, for the sake of precaution I never shook that bottle upright, so that if there was something inside it then it better remained at the bottom.

I returned the bottle and went ahead; after a quick check on my family I tried to revisit my precocious sleep. But, suddenly I got a notification (indication) from my urinary bladder that I had to excrete the urea out of my system. The sensation of it was quite violent and vibrant; thereby I was off the stairs within no time looking for a private clumsy space on the bus which I never got.

Therefore, I had to disturb the tobacco man again; I tried to oblige him so that he could have pulled the brakes, however, he was reluctant to do so; his argument was that the bus would stop in 5 minutes then I could do whatever and however I wanted to do it. Though, I wasn't pleased by it, the bumps in me were trying to crash my skin and get out of the bus, so I forced him, and he had to assent.

'Not more than two minutes or else I shall run away.' He said, this time more clearly. For a moment I thought that I should make him repeat his syntax in front of my guardians although, as a well brought up kid I didn't wake them up, for it would have disturbed the balance of my Karma. I was reckoning all of it in my own mind until the tobacco man spoke again with red particles flying off his mouth, 'What are you taking you urine back ?If that is even possible!' he continued. 'Get it out of the system; I have to rush like anything.' I didn't know how to even reply, therefore, I simply nodded my head thus bestowing him to proceed and hit the brakes. I feared his statement but not more than its implication, so I set a two minutes alarm in my conscious which would not please him to leave the ground.

The moment he stopped the bus all the adjacent eyes were on me, either they were astonished by the sudden break of the flow or they were frightened by a mere thought of accident! Although, they all inquired and came to know that that stoppage's reason was a child's willingness to pee. Some, got back to sleep while the others accused him for his act, and asked him that, 'how much time it would take if every individual get a separate time to pee?' The driver apologized to each and promised not to stop until we reached Haridwar.

I was looking at it all throughout and as fast as the one sided dispute was over the driver stared at me like a wolf. 'Go on, now!' he exclaimed with an angry expression but deep in him was a feeling of rhetorical anguish. I was off the vehicle in seconds where I hurried to find a place and I got the right place for it, therefore I proceeded towards it.

The beautifying atmosphere was as gorgeous as a belle, the aroma, and the marveling approach of that inspirational morning scenario was superlative! But I could hardly grasp those lovely moments as my eyes refused to open up. I was blind folded by the amount of light entering into my eye balls. I was walking in vain with both my eyes and conscious closed, where else the urinary bladder about to open!

With no turn whatsoever I walked straight towards the wall where the task which I was going to attempt was banned, but the voice of stereotypical thinking pushed me towards it, with no intension of resisting it.

"BAM!" a voice came, perhaps from the lower end of the road, however I knew that I had ran onto a small pole, but I merely wanted to see how bad it was. Blood! It was all round by my leg, the wounds were deep, though, some would have loved to contradict my observation. But, no one could sense the cavalry I was in, both my eyes got wide opened and they would never close even if I was willing to do so. The walk of a lion got converted into a rat walk-where one puts his hand on his knees and tries to move forth with unwilling and anguishing expressions!

Though, I made it till there, somehow. Still, the problems kept thrashing me; I opened my zip with a sudden intention, but the problem of it was that it was very difficult to pee when you were in pain! Never could I felt it coming, it seemed to me as a false alarm thus I ended up regretting my call.

I had to close my zip instantly for I had this alarm banging all over my head, but I heard a huge amount of sound coming from my back which pressurized me to take a look at it. While turning I had both confusing and fearsome instinct over my senses.

As I rotated my front to 180 degree, I nearly had a cold stoke in addition with a heart attack. The underrated bus in which I was travelling was ravished and crushed away with a bang by a TRUCK which was speeding unlimitedly! Not even a single sound part of the bus could be seen, only the freshly dilapidated metal parts were the highlight of the scenario. For a second, I lost myself, completely. Only a part of me was living which didn't let me have my faith in it, which would never permit me to leave the place, it was all DELUSIONAL according to him. It all seemed to me as a part of mixed and gigantic phenomenon, which was going to take place. The nearly occurred cardiac arrest had captured me from all ends and it wouldn't even let me lean ahead; but I had to go and check; for my family was out there, MY LIFE was out there!

I could evenly grasp the uncertainty of my lungs, the unruly behavior of my pulse and the mild nature of my frozen blood, as I took a step closer to the accidental site.

Tears started rolling out from my eyes for I could clearly see the drops of blood stained on the road, the broken glass pieces and the highly damaged metal. I kneeled on the road, where the small pieces of glass gently stabbed my skin thus entering my wounds, but I never cared, I was mingled in perhaps the biggest grief of my life! IT WAS LIKE MY WORST NIGHTMARE, coming into terms.

Accordingly, I saw a sharp white light gazing towards me and expanding as it came closer and closer, for it was something massive racing towards me with a ferocious speed. There was no stopping it I wanted to get out of the frame but the agony for the loss my precious ones and the trivial pieces of glass pulled me back, with no escaping howsoever!

I knew my end had came the mighty God of DEATH hath came! My legs were stuck on its place as if it were tied with some iron chain! I surrendered at last, and closed my eyes to welcome my fate and death toward me. IN ACCEPTANCE OF THE DENIAL!

8

"It doesn't matter if there is a life after death what does matter is if you are alive before death!"

My eyes fluctuated for it seemed quite burdensome to open them. I thought I had received the biggest present of my AFTER LIFE! For the place seemed to me as heaven and I did believe it then, blindly. Due to the contrast level of the place I determined to open my eyes gradually, as opening them at one go could have proven inevitable. But to whom was I kidding? I was already dead! How much more terminal could have proven in my afterlife?

Still, I opened them as slothfully as possible, where I could utterly espy a wooden strip in front of my eyes! 'Wood in heaven? So much for development!' I said to myself. I was unanticipated, confused and terrified at the same moment. 'Looks as if "they" took me through another route to reach this whole new destination; HELL!' I pleaded to myself. I was affrighted by the mere thought of it and the typical Indian facts, made it worse. "They feed you to the horrifying animals and then list your name in their menu followed by you getting eaten up by demons, prior to that you shall be subjected to a long dip in a hot oil tub!" I recalled. It scared the hell out of me and that too in Hell!

However, I never objectified this assumption as I knew my Karma balance was not in touch with the desired demand which could have categorized my name in there.

Though, as I further opened my eyes I saw some scenes which were familiar to my conscious. The pink colored wooden strip embedded with a brown colored paint was the wood in site, I reckoned my assumptions again which was followed by the to and fro movement of my neck, curiously setting up the desire to know if I was alive or not, by any means?

And, astonishingly I concluded my presence which was in the upper trunk of a bus going to Haridwar!

"Bad dreams are sometimes an intuition of the future!" For a bad dream it had become. I sat for some serious seconds, perpetually sighed in a couple of them and went to my slumber again, some would have wondered my valiant and composed behavior but then, I knew myself for sixteen long years, I knew that these bad dreams of mine would never come alive!

Therefore, I tried to sleep and for some reason or the other I found it reluctant either because of my dream or its corresponding instincts. 'What if it was all a trailer of the forthcoming future? What if all of this actually happens?' I asked myself.

'And, what if I save them; ALL OF THEM! People would appreciate me and my heroic tale; I'd long be heard in the ears of my forthcoming generation! They would commend my intuitional capacity or sixth sense to be, precise'. Though, this particular way of thinking of my senses was largely molded by a movie that I saw on the previous night of my departure, hence the effect was seen. I could have easily called myself a "Spinal cordless creature" for I had no firm belief in my own notions; but why would I?

"The fictional movie mania" of the previous night had authorized its copyright all over my nerves, therefore, I had to bend by back and sit straight, so I did. I woke up my father to deliver him my little but fatal dream!

I shook his back a couple of times, though quite briskly and then waited for him to get up and listen my bit. He looked at me strangely with horridly worried expressions. Quite, manifestly he got up however I didn't care about his uncomfortably disturbed morning routine for his sleep wasn't as weighty as our DEATH!

I confronted my little dream quite amusingly while he set a perfect parental byspel (example) by hearing me out with his sublime expressions, and as I finished my bit with a collective lot of sighs; 'It was just a bad dream.' He concluded with a yawn. 'Oh! But what if it was an intuition? Shall we go forth, on such risky terms? (The terms being a dream)' I asked on top of my voice. 'Well, we will go forth and not a thing will happen, you shall see.' He pleaded, while he thought for a couple of minutes. 'You said that the bus had an accident when it was still, right?' 'Yes, but...' I stammered. 'Then, for your information the bus will not stop for a moment and it had already gone past its desired time (looking at his watch) and THEY (the drivers) have to make it on time or else their payment will get off! So get your head down and relax (gets back to his original position) do not over think about such dreams.' He finished while turning his body on the other side.

I was doomed! Once again, my hands were tied with knots by my own father with his expertise skills of orating and persuading the opposite end; which were better than that of a women.

The protagonist mode was switched off within the blink of a speech; I had to drink the spiteful and diluted form of reality. I never could sleep again in that bus not merely because of the harsh truth but also the pungent fragrance from the adjacent compartment which was probably of an elderly smelled local woman. I felt like puking for a second although I had to consume it backwards with the spiteful and diluted form of reality. For a remedy, I kept my face out the whole time so that I could have abstained the smell of it which was literally driving me crazy!

The arrival time was derived as 11 o' clock by the local passengers the previous night, while then it was 11:30 and still our entreated place (Haridwar) was nowhere near the corner. We were displacing inch by inch, as sluggishly as possible. Some in favor, which were perhaps the isolated group of people, presented their argument with the logic of a "traffic jam" collected on the outskirts of the city or maybe, some random cow was delivering her "holy calf" or there could have been an accident and both the contenders of the respective vehicles would have been quarreling on the streets thus triggering the amount of delay.

When the in force party was asked he gave the time limit as twenty minutes but that was an hour before the then reported present time which was 1 o' clock.

"Waiting is a calm and composed task but the excess of it would ultimately leave you furious!" However, the patience level of my father was something commendable, he answered my exactly same question every time with a time interval of two minutes, which precisely was, 'When will we reach?'

9

So finally we were in Haridwar and it took me a deadly dream, three hours of sleep and 14 hours of uneasiness to reach in there.

After an hour or so we arrived in our, "family booked hotel" which in actual terms was nowhere close to even a half a star hotel. Basically, it was just a '10 roomed' flat with rats and flies all around and dirt was a common embellishment. There were no beds and we had to sleep on the mattresses which were spread on the despicably cracked and disgusting floor. For more, it was rather a 'Dharamshala' with a delusional name 'Hotel' written on its entrance board.

As soon as we landed our suitcases on the mattresses with a pitiful bed sheet spread on it in a haphazard way we made our minds up to get a cup of tea which would take our exertion away within one sip, however it was served after an hour and in addition it became an 'ice tea' due to the delayed delivery.

After the rough tea session we all decided to take a bath but the shameless manager refused to provide us any water for there was nothing left in the outlet and quite valiantly they suggested us to transfer our bathing session to the river Ganga! It was quite an embarrassment for us to stay in there but we had to. Although, as for our bath was concerned we found it pretty reasonable to dive into the river, it could not have been better for us if we started our stay with a concordantly confined soul embedded with the purest water on the planet!

But the question was, 'how would we go?' our other relative was perceiving our discussion from a stretched end, and when we were in a state of rhetorical dilemma he advised us to wait for half an hour more as they (our family who were organizing this function) had hired some cars which would take us to Ganga! It sounded somewhat threatening to us on the first instance however we ended up applauding ATLEAST this little service from their end.

And, so we did linger though for one and a half hour MORE, then we decided to eat some grains for it would have taken us some time to arrive from there and till then we would have ended up starving, like a skeleton. Just after half an hour more we sat in to take our salt less food diluted with a huge amount of water and rotten quality oil.

Somehow, we eluded from the mess as quick as we heard a horn of a vehicle. All of us took our towels and adjusted our bowels for we were all set to dive into the HOLIEST RIVER of the entire universe!

'Are we ready?' asked the driver enthusiastically. 'Ho! We are.' We exclaimed as we sat on our seats pretty drastically. 'Har Ki Pauri'- called as the capital mark of Ganga was about 4 miles away from our stay and then there was some festive season going on at that time of the year which more or less extended the time and distance it was going to take us to reach in there.

'So, finally we are here, eh?' My grandfather said with his dominating tone. 'I remember....' my father intervened while scratching his head, 'There is a myth! Ah, about this place that when the God's were quarreling with the demons for a vessel full of the 'immortalizer' both the sides were stretching the vessel with an intense force and somehow 4 drops accurately four drops fell onto four different places on the earth and amongst them was this place, 'Har Ki Pauri.' 'So, that means that this place is immortal?' I curiously asked while coming onto the edge of my seat. 'Yes! God himself cannot make it mortal! And, for the same reason they say that this water purifies and immortalizes your soul!' he said with an erudite tone. 'I have always heard many a times that this water washes away all our sin?' my brother enquired. 'No! It doesn't work that way it is sorely a wrong way of interpreting it. SINS are our Karma that we perform and nothing can erase them! They say that when we enter into this holy stream the "water" acts as a detoxifying agent. It takes away all your diseases and morally it gives you an internal energy or power which never allows you to do 'Sins' again, but up until you are purely determined. Everyone commits sins but the quantity and quality of it make you differentiated!' my father explained.

'But these days our "Ganga Ma" is rather giving skin diseases, to some!' The driver said, jumping into our conversation. 'Yea! The water level has gone down a bit and its quality has dilapidated in the near past. But to say that the river is making people sick is rather a wrong to way to look at things; the water comes clean with a good persisting flow, till now! But, due to these dams and dirt coming from almost all the corners things are getting worse. It is we who demean it and it is we who suffer, as simple as that! There is no role of the river it just consumes what we engulf!' my uncle concluded. 'Talking environment now, are we?' my grandfather asked as he was talking with the other passengers.

The driver parked the vehicle as we prolonged our discussion. 'And, here we are gentlemen!' said the driver while taking the key out of his vehicle. 'I don't see any river here?' my brother asked with a confused voice. 'Oh! Sire, you got to walk for that a bit, the river is on that opposite end.' The driver spoke while pointing his finger towards the river. 'Well, let's get out, we need to walk some distance, right?' My uncle said as he stood out of the door.

Well, we WAULKED a lot that noon, things got more complicated, as for, we had to drop our slippers in the car itself so that no one applies the EXHANGING OFFER OF A SLIPPER.

Stones were thrashing our feet and the anguish of it could have been effortlessly felt in the lower ends of our toes while hopping (walking).

On our lateral sides we saw some stalls where many antique items were sold including the old currency which was obsolete in those days with some old Indian toys and handicraft; on the very same instance we saw some destitute in the frame as well, however, we were occupied enough to care as then the dense sunlight was stabbing our feet's cell.

At last we arrived at the 'Har Ki Pauri' after having some serious harm in our legs; it felt as if we were subjected to one thousand nails heated on the furnace with cruel intentions.

Our first task was to visit a nearby temple and so we bent our heads down in there for one could have easily clasped the presence of a huge river flowing with a tremendous velocity. As we were getting close to the river a divine soul was gradually alluring me into its arms, the cold breeze was overwhelming and the moist air was one of its kinds!

I stood in front of the river where a huge rabble was detoxifying their KARMA, hoping to clear the old sins and attempting some new ones. The whole crowd was unbelievably naked and the next moment I found my family members in the religious river sensing, feeling and drinking the HOLY WATER!

My father waved a hand toward me thus inviting me into that chilling and freezing water. Although, I refused for I was not on top of my health and on a serious note I was scared by the fact that the water would give me some kind of skin disease! Then again, I was given a rescuing hand by my father for he told me that this water would take my dizziness away rather than making me ill. And, I had to believe him also I knew that he won't misguide me by any means!

Once again, I got persuaded by my own father to step into the river. Pretty willfully and forcefully I moved my leg an inch ahead towards the water. "Holy crap!" were my instantaneous words and white did my face go simply after touching it, I withdrew my feet back and sat on the nearby step thus watching "them" enjoy. Though, then again I was forced to re-enter into the stream for then my brother had accused me for being a "school girl"!

It was cold! Oh, it was! But, once I worked my way in it felt good and we remained in there for hours; the water was truly purifying it gave us an alleviating experience; our soul had a proper definition then, as if it was the only bath we needed in our lives with each of its dip came an internal energy and with each sip came liability. There was no one to take us out of the river until the 'Aarti'- a prayer session, came into force.

For 'Aarti' everyone had to come out of the river as it would then impugn the divine nature of Ganga and so they did, quite willingly.

We sat on the steps adjacent to us so that we could have watched the minting and enticing session; everyone had their cameras, one which would help them to rewind their contentment and one which would help them to feel their live presence of that rejuvenating site, whenever they would like!

There were merely two sounds echoing in that atmosphere one was of the "BELLS" and the second one was of the "quick stream flow". The lighted lamp which was diving in the river due to a lot of vibrant rotation looked as if the stars were falling onto the mass. The positivity was built up all around the river bed and we took it with us into our souls and went away by the shore just as to sense the wind coming towards us. On our way, I heard a couple of natives talking about the bad weather conditions in "KEDARNATH"- A religious hub of Lord Shiva. And also how unusual it was!

We went straight into our car and sat in it to take a good night sleep, though, before that we hoped for a good night meal, which we never did get!

The food was pitiful and certainly a waste of efforts that time again, my parents weren't satisfied with the provided facilities and they were chatting with each other in our room about the amenities just as my family members arrived and they too felt a room for improvement. 'We should pack our luggage and shift to a new hotel, I will pay!' My aunt said. 'Well, we all appreciate your gratitude but it is not about money rather it is about the relationship. How would they feel when they will come to know about this, that, just because of our superiority we left this hotel to satisfy our luxurious thirst?' my grandfather explained.

Thereby, out of our parental love and relationship we had to stay there alone, amongst all the stickiness, stinking and mosquitoes 'God! Burn them!' I prayed in my own tone every time they irritated me.

Somehow between scratching and itching we crossed our night and got prepared for the other to attend the function. The level of sanitary facility just kept falling with the increment in the number of guests coming to attend the function.

So, we all sat down to debate about various topics including politics, new generation, me getting scolded and were proceeding even further. Abruptly, the topic changed to 'THE FOUR DHAMS' — these were the four religious places of the earth where each and every Hindu tried to visit once in their life time in search of peace and calmness in their life. These were rather similar to that of the other religions, just the place changed and so did the name. 'We are here now! So why not? Let's go!' My uncle said. Most certainly he said it so as he could maintain the tropical flow of the conversation but the others took him seriously. 'But how can we go? We got no arrangements? No clothes? And, no gas?' my aunt enquired. Once again our relative was hearing the conversation and he suggested us that there was a clothing agency nearby which picked up clothes or luggage from our place and delivered it to "the desired place". Furthermore, there was an ATM on the other end so we could get our bucks from there and accordingly hit the gas. Some did contradict the hasted call while the others called their cabs! And majority of them were ready thereby creating a win-win situation for me.

Fortunately, my grandmother was at home, so we called her up to beseech her to join us but she refused for the same reason; but then we obliged her to bundle our entire luggage and submit them in the "luggage agency". To my misfortune, only my jacket, jeans and a sweater were selected since she didn't know the formats of the official suits and cloth.

Somehow, I started regretting that we had to attend the family function for which we came here, as our trunk full of materials would arrive anytime in the next morning plus we had to hire a vehicle which would take us to our destination.

And, so we attended our function which in precise term wasn't that much intriguing! It was as normal as a clerk's job, nothing especial; all the daily routine rituals performed quite NORMALLY!

However, we were then completely put to go on a life trekking experience, no disturbance and no formalities. Though, I knew that some of my teenage friends would have disliked the notion about going onto such religious places however for me it was a platinum opportunity, which I would haven't missed for a cause.

Later that night, we found a travelling agency which assigned us our vehicle to travel upon; our agent talked to some guy for a few minutes then he told us about the condition of the vehicle which according to him was well in touch, had a nice interior, comfort on the whole and it was a 'good to go in' vehicle.

Then we had some fine dinner on our way back perhaps the paramount of the ones which we were going to experience in the forthcoming days.

We arrived at our 'Dharamshala' and it so happened that we found people leaving the place which for us was a good sign, many beds got empty then and we slept in an "AC affiliated" room which were not provided to us previously.

We woke up the next morning and found our luggage in front of us since our relative was kind enough to pick them up from the station or agency. I saw my darling clothes and tried them on so that I could have accurately noticed the fault. Quarter to twelve we were all prepared to visit the four religious sites.

The driver was called before 12 o' clock, till then we had to finish our lunch, get our dresses on the correct places, take all are money required money off as it was at last going to be divided between all of us excluding our grandfather; and my other uncle would keep a track of it. Also, we kept all are meds and pills in our pocket so that we could be called 'Precaution' beings.

The clock passed 12:15 right away and there wasn't any indication of our vehicle. We called in to ensure if he was appearing or not. Although, soon a vehicle grey colored, old, pungent and driven by an unfit guy arrived.

We glanced at it steadily and sensed the irony coming. The interior of the vehicle which had become an old SUV was more ironical than the previous. There was no auto staring, the seats had springs and sponges hoping out of it and also he had no music in his car!

We somehow modified our luggage pretty indecently and moved our waists to get into that car, apprehensively!

10

The weather was humid, fertile, clouds up on top, sun was almost out of the cloud's blanket glaring in a deep way, birds had their airplane mode on and it looked as if a whole new troposphere was created!

I rotated my neck out of the window to get a check on the ongoing wind. 'Hey! Get your face in kid!' a voice as loud as a matured man appeared. The wind blowing outside turned into a cold stream. 'Don't you know how dangerous it is to keep your head out of the vehicle? You might get sick or for better you might just get your head chopped off either by another pair of wheels or a mountain.' my father warned. And, I had to make a vow for not to repeat that again up until my brother started doing it too and I had no control over me so I mimicked him but when unexpectedly I saw a car coming toward me with a tremendous speed willing to chop my head, I withdrew my head from there while I felt dead for a moment. The theory of a Parent's scolding always proves it right or so I reckoned and got aware of. "Sometimes when we consider that our parents won't prove a helping hand in our important life decisions they just do, somehow. And, they are indeed right every time, for more, the only mechanism which is perfect in this entire universe is a Parental mechanism!"

We all felt our stomach water gliding for we were travelling through those venerating mountain ranges and soon we reached to this place named 'Dehradun"- a hill station which was always a topic of discussion for anyone who crossed through Rishikesh to get in here. Rishikesh again had some internal beauty of its own for some reason.

Some of us began vomiting until we reached another hill station known as "Mussorie". The elevation of those mountains caused our ill health. The car was unsuitably distasteful and the elevation further added to our misfortune. My father wasn't evenly contended but that was durable enough to take control of his acid reflux unlike my other relative who vomited, sorely.

Puking or its feeling could have only be braked by hawking the black peppered mint pills which proved quite beneficial for us on the first place while "terminal" for us in the morning.

Our first stop was Yamnotri- the first Dham of the four. Quite gritty to climb and even obstructing to reach. And, it wasn't possible to reach directly in there on the first day itself as we had to trek for the whole way with our legs since no vehicle was allowed in the inner premises also it was getting dark then. So, we determined to start our route on the other day, early in the morning.

Till then, we kept our suitcases in the nearby hotel which was in fact better than the previous one. The walls were moist and frosty which could have ultimately allowed the chilled wind to enter in the rooms. But, it was already dark then and we were lazy enough to check onto another. For we were tired of both puking and traveling; it was essential for us to take some respite.

My mother took the charge of standing and bargaining in such conditions; as women were more comfortable with it than men. I don't remember how much it took us to spare our while in there but it was virtually in our budget.

We revamped our materials thus fixing them and getting both people and things right on their places. While some of us kept our trunks aside and ran away in the washroom the others changed and got into their shelter briskly.

As soon as we could have brought tomorrow's plan into consideration we found ourselves sitting in the mess and eating, chance wise. The food obviously was, ridiculous, it had no odor, taste and moreover it caused 'Peptic ulcers' to some of my elders.

After all the ingesting and burping we sat and be talked about planning things for the next morning however we ended up debating about the entire schedule of our journey, which was-:

DAY 1: travelling for YAMNOTRI.

DAY 2: Arrive at YAMNOTRI and then start progressing for GANGOTRI.

DAY 3: Reach GANGOTRI and then take a day off to travel and look at SITES.

DAY 4: Sit in the vehicle and begin proceeding for KEDARNATH.

DAY 5: Strike KEDARNATH and visit the temple.

DAY 6: From KEDARNATH starts extending towards BADRINATH.

DAY 7: Visit the temple and from there go back to HARIDWAR.

DAY 8: Stay in a hotel, get some lunch and then wrap up.

DAY 9: BACK TO HOME!

But, things never happen according to our plans!

11

After setting the blueprint of the trip right we conversed about how to get on top? YAMNOTRI was one of those lengthy and exerting temples which was located at a distance of 7 miles from the origin. In addition, the path to the top of the temple was dead slanting, if something was dropped from the top of the temple it would have either ended in the river 'YAMUNA' or it would have stopped directly at the origin that too if it was so fortunate enough. The path was constrained, on one side of the mountain channels while on the other side there was a huge and deep valley where the river 'YAMUNA' used to flow and still flows!

The next moment I found myself on the origin of the temple where a long lane of four wheeled vehicles were trying to enter the premises at least some of them desired so while not a single one of them could achieve. Our driver recommended us to take the terrestrial route due to the long and huge crowd of the vehicles it was nearly impossible to move it forth, thus, we got out of the car to cover up the distance on our own, legs.

So, there we were under our own steam to get to the initial stage and hence forth, instigate our journey. Though, the means on which we were going to travel wasn't thence determined. Seldom did my mother sat on a pony and even my velour father. These ponies lied candidly in between horses and donkeys they were the middle most figure of it and majority of them astoundingly were bisexual!

My mother didn't permit me to steam it by my foot rather she asked me to complete my journey on a pony, as for, the rest of my cousins had already surrendered on the first place itself.

Nevertheless, with my open efforts I swayed my parents to let me trek the distance by my feet. Quite hardcore as that was! Not to say less, I was footing up to YAMNOTRI with my parents and a couple of relatives while the others were perceptibly on top of their relevant mammals.

My youngest cousin cried a lot, as for, his parents were leaving him for some hours persistently and he had to take on the route alone, excluding the pony and its driver. Although, my uncle comforted him and calmed his nerve by letting him know that he wasn't a solitary creeper.

And, so after making those all sit on a bisexual pony, unnervingly; we too decided to proceed our way on the initials.

We started steaming up the hill and tried to seize longer steps however not forgetting to straighten up our knees as it would have then costed us on the other night. My dad advised me to take the camera with me which would help us to capture our glorious moments and would let us recall these precious days, when we would be looking forward to it in the near future.

Although, there was this shop on the outskirts of the town of a stick which usually was used to trek high peaks however those were professionally thick and grapy while these were thin and worthless and so was their result.

But, some said that it would assist us to trek our way up to the temple and also it would give us a feeling of a professional mountaineer, including the mordantly elusive shop keeper.

My parents suggested us to be in touch while climbing and to walk almost vertically equal so that in any ill episode one could call the other and accordingly so. Although, after a minute, everyone flew away and got dispersed due to their differential velocities!

I was roughly two miles away from my mother, aunt and uncle who were searching for me all throughout the trip while I was all pumped with gas which would be sealed only when I reached onto the top of the temple. And, ironically I was exploring them that time around.

They tried to catch hold of me but they couldn't, somehow and ultimately I had to get to them while, they were seen in a condition completely conflicting with which they have begun.

Their sweat was on and lungs were excruciating like anything; my father gave me a hundred bucks to procure a glucose contained biscuit packet and also some cold drink to rest upon. Though, it costed more than what we expected that was more than hundred bucks; the shopkeepers used to sell items more than their MRP rates for they knew that to buy their products was an obligation since no single one could afford to bargain and we had to bestow against what they asked but what they deserve.

For at least four instances we clogged by to hawk some cups of tea but not me as it wasn't my cup of tea. Though, their healthy state was reducing to knots; one known reason was of the oxygen level present around the atmosphere which was fairly low than the surface level and it was merely going to get shoddier.

12

As I was just about my way up on my feet with thinner and sharper steps I felt a surge of adrenaline crossing through my veins- a lunatic pony was running towards me from my back and its front. My legs got jammed on its relevant place as If I was paralyzed and it had no escape!

I was toward the river side and there were no chances of me jumping to the other side for there were some couple of young men carrying a wooden stack around their heads and taking their parents onto that even if I had to shift towards that side it would have dismantled them then it could have been a gist of debacle. Also, it was rather fragile to bare one death than several of them.

I being a plucky combatant stood in attention and waited for my demise being my eyes bunged tightly. And, there I felt a hand coming towards me which pulled me in the middle zone of the path where I never reckoned of going. But, luckily that random person saved me from a legit occurrence.

All, I could grasp by my visual lens was a purple blazer with a white laced thread embraced on it and obviously a person wearing it which perhaps was a lady. Before, I could have captured the visage in my natural camera she had disappeared into the odds, leaving no trace behind her. And, her female characteristics could have been well noticed by her fairy and curvy hairs suspending down the aisle. However, the front portion remained a mystery for she raced her way up to the temple. For the rest of my voyage I trekked carefully and steeply!

But, as I peeped my way down the path I initiated my elders besieging their way up the aisle. My uncle was red as nothing but blood while my aunt was pale blue as frozen blood. "Facial expressions are a guide in itself!"

Though, my chief sense of duty was to let them cool down and vice versa to the ones who were wise vise versa. Their hemoglobin begged for oxygen, therefore, we had to desist and for innumerable times. However, those frequent stoppages made me edgy but then after looking at their state I had to alter my patience level.

Somehow, somewhere and with great difficulties we reached onto the halfway! But, then the duration made me furious and I determined to trek it over to the temple however reckoning the condition of my elders it included some check outs on them and a few stoppages for my own safety.

We considered grasping the nature's beauty as a crucial call but hardly could we see in the midst of both exertion and walking, nevertheless, it was the temple's outer atmosphere that got us going. The gentle little massage over our face and the child wind accompanied by the wet vapors of the river Yamuna were the descendants of our arrival!

After, that entire "workout"; we got to the temple within several hours and I sat adjacent to the temple behind the changing room as we all had to find our other relatives who departed several hours ago and once that was done we had to gather around for a holy bath in the hot steamed water. Thence, my parents made me be seated with all our clothes so that I could keep an eye on them.

While sitting, I sensed my head burning like a furnace with me pressing it with a specific thrust. There was this guy who sat adjacent to me and the people used to call him a "healer". So, he promised me to take charge of the headache while our conversation was taking place and also he was noticing my hand actions so he vowed to fade way my headache by his Godly powers. And, I had no better alternative so I opted to go with him and this is what "SOME" doctors did, basically. "Pinch the weak nerve and attain all their money!"

'Close your eyes!' he said. I with no odds to choose kept following his commands. He kept his hand on my forehead and pinched it with a gentle gesture; I was regretting my decision of letting him touch my body but then, 'What shall a dying being do?' I calmed myself.

'Now, you can open them.' he said and with a douching expressions while I unbolted them. 'Can you feel anything?' he asked. 'Any headache or any sort of pain?' he continued. And, BAM! The pain was gone and it really felt fine; it was better than any sort of medication that I have ever had! It was real quick, like a marvel actually more superior and practical than it.

I praised him for his wonderful gift of healing and I requested him to do the same with my "in suffering" relative(s). However, he repudiated as he had to take an urgent flight from that place and so he flew.

Sometime later I felt something hard and crusty banging my head as a desperate salesman; it was my headache and it had entered again after taking a U-turn.

He was cunning, and sharp were his tricks; but for me he was nothing less than a con practicing a hand on his next client; I checked my pockets and I found out that they were bare, he had taken it all, however, after sometime I realized that I had nothing in it. And, so I settled with a headache!

Although, all my praising him had transformed into accusing within a blink of an eye that he got me to do in his obscene therapy.

13

Out of the blues, I saw my father walking toward me, 'We can't find your brother!' He said. 'Which one?' I asked. 'The tall one off course!' he added. 'Your uncle and your brother arrived here an hour ago, but we can't find them, now.' He continued. 'Wait! Both of them? And, where possibly could they be? It's not a huge place, is it?' I asked. He waited by instantly and stared at the place deeply, 'Exactly! You took my line; now, get your heads up and move to the bathing place but REMEMBER JUST HURRY UP! As that water contains a good amount of Sulphur and if you don't do it quickly then you might just faint, your aunt almost fainted!' he concluded by guiding my way toward the bathing tank or pool I supposed.

The water was in fact soothing and once I got in it there were no chances which could have got me out of there, except my father and his fear to be more precise.

He pulled me out of there and made me change my clothes within some minutes for it would have impinged on my health.

'Just wait in here for some time I will grab your mom and the others in here.' He said and disappeared into the crowd. And, so once again I sat with utter lucidity and at the same time a bit of oddity for there were people who came from the various parts of the country and luckily I found this girl from Bangalore who was sitting beside me. She didn't know Hindi and I didn't know English, at least not that much but then it being a superior language and as some remarked it as a language of intellect; I had to speak up to her, for only English would present my personality as a better one unlike my mother tongue. And, there were various translators too standing up to the cue and aiding her to converse with the local people.

'Ah, Where are y-you fro-from?' I stammered. 'Bangalore.' She added with her Bengali accent. We tried to debate on various topics including the weather, hot springs and she did know a lot and I knew it as, I was diving further and further into that tête-à-tête conversation however my other uncle saw me and as some random fifth grader he mocked me for it throughout the whole trip.

'Let's visit the temple, shall we?' he sarcastically asked. 'Yes, please!' I said with an embarrassing tone as I stood up. The next moment we started walking towards the temple and I turned back to wave a hand toward her, however, she preferred to ignore.

We went to the temple and the line was scanty. The temple looked similar to that internet photograph which I saw before my departure from Jaipur. There I saw all the four places it wasn't planned but I had this project to execute thereby I looked at them from the outer angle as the inner one wasn't available.

It seemed quite normal from the outer side for much I had done to reach in there and astoundingly it was a common looking temple, however, I couldn't recall going inside it.

Some seconds later, I found my aunt yelling about something; I went close to give an ear and successively I could see her eyes numb and swollen, perhaps, because of crying. She was accusing my uncle as he took her son away who on special notice was asked to take care of him. At last, they concluded with a certainty of finding them near the parking which was down the place as they might have ended up there. But, surely it did take the fun out of it!

We moved towards the departure area and started gazing at the unlimited valley and the limited slanting path way. Everyone accepted the proposal of going down by their feet excluding the kid, elders and injured ones. I gave a positive response onto that one, though, then my parents got firm and said, 'You have done a magnificent job walking that far; it's definitely commendable but then slanting down seven more miles will not be piece of cake and it will make you sick, already your immunity is similar to nowhere. And, you will not be able to visit the other temples, so, get onto that pony and wait for us downwards, try to find your brother, perhaps.' They explained. I had to bend my head beneath their instructions for I had my point to prove and I completely did that.

They hired a pony soon and made me sit on it; in addition, they told me to hang around the parking are as they might get late.

Getting on top of that pony was a colossal task! However, somehow with the help of my parents and the pony's driver I managed my way up to its back. Where else my other relative almost fell from it while getting up.

And, so they began scampering down the path as if they had sensed an earthquake however there wasn't one; the driver said that it was their original pace.

My other aunt suggested me to stay in touch with her and don't run away like I usually do, as if it was in my hands!

Things worsened on the lateral turns for those ponies weren't an automated machine they had also adopted the biological machinery inside their bodies and so they used to function by their moods sometimes quick and running while the other times trivial and hanged.

'It would have been much better if I had sat on a bull instead of this mad animal!' I said to myself, every time it created an issue which was either stopping instantly at its place or running around like psychotic beings. In addition, those death eaters had names too; mine was "Chetan" while the one of my aunt was "Bhagat"!

It took me half the time and double the uncomforting duration to reach the "parking place" or the initial place from where we had began our expedition.

During the ride, I was free enough to chatter with my pony's driver cum care taker. 'So, do you go to school?' I enquired while developing the lead journalist feeling inside me. 'No! We don't have time for that, there (pointing towards a mountain) I live, and there (pointing towards some other mountain) is the school and here (looking towards me) I am.' 'So, how much do you ah get?' I asked while maintaining the journalist feeling inside me. But, for an instance I thought that he would advice me to mind my own business, so, I backed out of the conversation.

'750 bucks per day, it's very difficult for us to buy our own pony, and so we take them on rent and get paid. However, someday I will own my private pony; not one, but all of them this "Chetan" that "Bhagat" will be fully mine no half.' He answered. Such little fantasies he had in his mind; I thought that his life was an ideal one but there comes the irony into play. He was also 16 and he used to get up early in the morning to drive people up and down 14 miles here and then 28 in Kedarnath but surely they used to cross it more than one time. And, here we were whining about only 7 miles with no one to take care of.

All of that and possibly more just to get 750 bucks? Well, it sounded pretty reasonable to me at first although when I discovered that he had no parents my maturity level and the love for my guardians dropped out of my eyes. "For, it's really not about how we are born it's about how we die!"

Maybe someday he would pursue his ambition or perhaps someday he would expand his ambition!

14

We had to wait for two long hours and I was dead tired as I got to the "parking place". There wasn't any sign of our vehicle in which I could have rested, also, I never got any kind of seat to comfort my body; we (me and my other aunt) were in deep vexation and we made several announcements on the mike so that they could trigger their walking velocities after hearing them. However, they never cared for they came down with their original pace. And, it indeed costed us a lot of pain!

At last, we all met and astonishingly we found my brother and the uncle resting in the vehicle which was parked at a hideous spot, which was quite difficult to explore! And, as it was later elaborated by my uncle that the boy was coughing badly and he had some signs of giddiness, in addition, there was no means of communication. So, he determined fairly to bring him down to the plain and get him a bite to eat which then was followed by him lying down inside the vehicle which was asked to be parked under a shady spot so that he can get cured lucidly.

All the "aggression" of my aunt got melted by degrees and she even greeted a "Thank you" for taking such good care of him and fulfilling his promise. "Adults sometimes act as hypocrites!"

We all sat comfortably well this time around as for our stored fat got reduced into goods. Some had it reduced by walking others did it by simply sitting on the uprising ponies while exceptions like me preferred to get it done by dipping hands in both the buckets.

We arrived at our two roomed hotel by 6:00 PM and we started traveling for GANGOTRI; while during the roving we confabulated about how things shaped themselves and how silly we were to give up the enjoyment, also, we chattered about how that ride on pony was and how shall we prepare stuff for KEDARNATH!

The effect of winter and cold atmosphere increased by three folds as we arrived near this town, "HARSIL" which was famous for its implausible water fall and where also some "Bolly-wood" movies were shot in the early 80s.

We made our minds up to visit the place, however, firstly we were advised to put some more woolen cloth on our bodies and ironically the one who advised us himself got cold stricken and sadly, it was my dad! I found him shivering and shaking down the line and especially sneezing as it was the first symptom we noticed before our medical conclusion.

After looking at certain random hotels we checked into one of those coldest hotels of all simply as it matched our budget. But, this time around I didn't criticize it, for all I could care about was of my father's health.

When a thermometer was provided to us it was initiated that his temperature got risen up by four degrees from the normal. Although, things got usual in the morning while it took my breath and slumber away for the whole night!

Next morning, I found myself sitting in the vehicle with my clothes wrapped inside my towel in one of my hands and some food articles in the other. Sometime later, I saw my family members sitting next to me as the driver ignited the engine for we left for the second DHAM, GANGOTRI!

15

GANGOTRI had its perks in itself; the place was dead cold and for the sake of religious purity you had to bathe in that ice cold river flowing nearby. It was factually ten times icier than the water we had encountered in HARIDWAR.

Some people believed that GANGA initiated its way from a cave named, "GO-MUKH" which was a mountainous cave formed in a structure similar to that of a cow. No one had ever seen it from the interior angle; few tried however they never could reach in there. And, how could have they? The flow of it was pretty brisk and no human or terrestrial organism could have withstood it! And, if some dope minded guy did get in, somehow, he never could have got back out.

Some believed that "GO- MUKH" would lead you way to the "Kailash Mountain" where Lord Shiva would guide your way to perpetuity! Although, some condemned its possibility for geographically, KAILASH Mountain was nowhere near it. Nevertheless, one point was damn clear behind that cave was pure and sure Eternity!

So, the water was accurately in negative figures as it used to come by the melting of glaciers which were not so much distant from the temple. For that made the water chilled and my heart cold!

The river was chilled and moving, in addition, we had to take a bath before we enter into the temple for those were the guidelines provided to us by the temple people so yup we were doomed!

The journey to the temple was delightfully pleasant as we had nothing to trek and cars were allowed till the outer end of the temple so all we had to do was to sit and bathe and then visit the temple, also, it was not that much away from where we were staying.

There were no miles to climb and no mad animals to lay our hips on however it was more reckless and treacherous than that. During, the way itself we were fortunate enough to get a good background which did boost up our photo session.

'And, here we are sire.' said the driver. We advised him to park the vehicle somewhere and come with us to the temple though he preferred to stay by his vehicle. And, so we got out of our shelters to take a long hard look at the premises.

The place was a real tourist attraction; they were all around the ground in the Indian suits and sarees. It was regrettable for me to look at the scenario as I thought that the foreigners suited well in the Indian tradition while we found ourselves comfortable in the continental clothes. There was a good amount of culture exchanged by two or more countries but again it set a fastidious example of a liberal world.

Then we arrived at the outer end of the temple however we were suggested to take a real quick bath in the holy river, as for, it would add onto the beauty of visiting this holy place.

We considered that there was no room for warm blooded and elderly people but to our astonishment the later one were diving and refluxing their arcs onto its most basic position and one was from my own family, my grandfather.

Nevertheless, the water was somewhat cleaner and purer as compared to the one we encountered in HARIDWAR; also some chains were provided so as to hang on to the river and not let yourself flow away since if one started flowing from here he would directly end up in the Bay of Bengal.

We had to sit on those old metamorphic rocks and pour the water mug by mug and so all of us went quite reluctantly to have a bath of a few mugs. That was the only one time except the previous one that I didn't prefer to touch the water surface; all of us bathed quite reluctantly but sure they did except me. I was hiding and sneaking around every time one called me up to get some of that holy water on my head.

Somehow, in the midst of hiding and niggling my mother explored me and she forcefully made me sit on a rock and poured water from that filthy little mug directly on my head. It was a complete shocking wave that passed onto my vertebral column and went to my optical nerve that blinded me for a second. Further, she handed me over the mug to continue my bathing process however the breeze was passing too swiftly which further added to my misfortune; and I sat on the rock dazzled and hanged with a filthy little metallic mug in my hand.

After, having a keen look at me, my brother complained against me to my mother for not pouring a mug onto myself. So, my mother came up to me and then again fetched some water from her own mug and poured the coldest, breath taking and Asthmatic water of all times; simply after two mugs I rushed to the nearest changing room which was a GHAT and picked up my towel to get dressed.

After, I got ready we had this Havan done from a local PANDIT (priest) which costed us a thousand bucks as his payment cum "DAKSHINA". But, as soon as the "Pooja"- prayer session got over I felt a sort of rigidness and addictiveness in my body as if I had lost it all and I felt short of breath; the oxygen level over there was fairly low and also the chilled water contributed to the lot which injected the temporary Asthma inside my body.

My family members surrounded me from all the eight sides which further triggered my dizziness; my parents gave me something which sort of cured me for a bit and I got my conscious back, right away. And, as soon as my eyelets got unlocked I found my father accusing me for being an immunity less kid and a person gifted with weak lungs, 'If your silly body can't tackle this then how will you make up till, Kedarnath?' he asked with a yelling tone. I had no answer and what would I probably say?

Where else, my mother assumed it as a false alarm she thought that I was faking it all; which in some terms was true. No one can escape from their mother's eyes. She imposed her faking thoughts on me and I had to defend myself; I had to cover all that and so I showed my aggression, for I stanched to not visit the temple that time!

However, my parents warned me not to exhibit my real face in front of the family members and be a good kid; I felt betrayed by my own parents but it was all temporary again as things got in shape till the next dawn. However, my teenage blues and belligerence on the same front didn't permit me to enter into the temple and I never did enter; but I did remember standing in a long line.

At last, after everyone was done looking at the God we roamed around the town and got a bite to eat at the adjacent café.

And, finally we sat in our vehicle and got back to our hotel where we packed our stuffs up and leaved for KEDARNATH!

16

It was day 3 and we had almost zipped our bag packs to departure for KEDARNATH, we sat in our old vehicle but similar to the first DHAM it was dark then and some held the opinion for waiting in the hotel itself while the others which were quite progressive in their own terms wanted to leave early so that we could have made it in time. KEDARNATH was 120 miles away from where we stood excluding the 14 miles of the pathway.

Thereby, we had to check out of the hotel and we determined ourselves to move towards the temple so that we could cover much distance, however, we had to stay in for that night in another hotel which was about 100 miles from the temple simply so that we could take some rest and get mentally equipped for the odds.

Although, there were some tribulations with it, we considered it a trip which was similar to that of YAMNOTRI but it wasn't so and we came to know about the real phase of it by our informative culprit, the driver, which made our concepts clearer and more dubious.

He started it up with the mythological name KEDARNATH which was assigned after the name Lord SHIVA and it was a historical temple which revolved its formation around a story which was of the time of MAHABHARAT.

However, he didn't know the story it had always been a debatable tale to talk about, but it indulged the urge in me to know about the story, I had always kept a fine place for mythological stories. It gave me a sense of reckoning each and every aspect of life in addition it was quite meriting, every time I had a curiosity in my mind about different phases of life I used to give an ear to the mythological parts.

It induced the knowing capacity in addition with some serious joules of energy in me and further it always ended giving up a moral lesson which was literally the superior part of it. So, I had to know about it at least the highlight of it for I could know where we were going.

Anyhow, the driver was full of facts. He was kind enough to shower his practiced lie on us but before that he made us imagined the temple and told us how emasculating and utterly God driven it was.

With it came the profit statement, 'KEDARNANTH is quite unreachable on the first day, it is 14 MILES AWAY, and that would be just the one way figure it becomes 28 when you roll down. Quite impossible for me to imagine someone coming down in one day and being clinically okay! It is really not up to my taste, I would rather suggest you to stay up in there for a night after walking up to it for then comfortably and composedly you can get a good look at Lord SHIVA. Afterwards, you can gently come back with a good suit on your shoulders and a delighting memory in your mind, you won't get these days back, will you?' the driver explained.

He was quite a salesman, he knew he would earn an extra bunch of bucks for his act and so he got to us and was able to dictate us and our entire timetable.

'So, we have to stay up there for a night? Don't you all realize how childish it is, and looking at the hotel conditions I am sure of the fact that we won't find a two starrer.' Said I. They lost their tongue, with my statement but due to their long experiences of such dilemma they knew how to backfire it.

'Yes, for a night! It is not reliable to come back medically safe as some of us might be travelling from our legs, so it will be risky for all of us; we have to continue our journey too. And, suppose if someone gets sick due to exertion then where will we cure him/her? There is no such facility at all. And, coming to the hotel fact it would be just a matter of one single night I think we can adjust our selves for choosing this would be more reliable and beneficially comfortable for us as we can accurately have HIS presence in our souls for a much longer duration, it would be worth your uneasiness.' My father encountered.

'But still, let us see it will depend upon the situation.' My mother said, thus relaxing both the ends.

Though, I didn't give up I called for polling, again. Only my energetic mother and I agreed upon the situation while the others never cared to disturb their ligaments. It was sad, really they fought their argument in the name of my grandfather, who was aged and it was pretty hard for him to make it up.

I had to surrender there was no option, and when we were finished the culprit driver had this internal smile in him which only I could notice, the others were blind folded by his skills of communicating. Where else, for me he was a cheap thief who had booked an extra charge from us.

17

We stopped by our hotel which was fairly a landscape in itself, it had the beautiful steps of terrace farming, roads were clean, no one to poke and behind the hotel there was a sheen curvature of a huge mountain.

But, before pulling the brakes we visited the capital of those mountain ranges, UTTARKASHI. The place was warm and humid, with 307 Kelvin on the board. We could observe our chin rising from the blanket as we were wearing it since GANGOTRI but here things were suitable and we could enjoy our bit.

I recalled my father telling me a story about how fortunate he was to leave the capital just some moments before, a disaster. He had visited the capital some time back perhaps in the 90s where the place was hit by a major earth quake driving towards the whole region. It annihilated the place and made it inevitable for residing. However, the trademark of it could never be found during my visit, it was a visit able site. Though, the memories couldn't faint themselves like the cracks; people weren't oblivious of the past calamities at all.

Intriguingly, our driver used to reside in that part of the country, he made us look at his home which was not in a delightful condition then he took us to a free tour of the city. Also, he made us glance at the piece of land that he used to own. The place was located near the pavement of a river, and he with his uncle had planned to hold a restaurant on that land.

Although, the land wasn't reliable at all! It stood on the outer end of a fast flowing river which was prone to floods and things. The deal wasn't flexible; it took his annual salary to pay the first installment of the land loan and still there was a continuous fear for that land as it could have been easily driven away by the merely present vital forces surrounding the atmosphere.

When he was enquired about the risk factors he gave an unbelievable response which in his words was, 'I am not frightened by any such dark forces, there are many and we have seen a lot and we are indeed prepared for the worst. The river would take its turn someday and we will have to surrender, all of us have to! But, it doesn't mean that we should nurture fear in our hearts about things which are going to come, and we are perhaps not sure of it. We (driver) believe in living once so why should we care about a mere piece of land? It is all in Lord SHIVA'S hand. HE would let us in and only HE would let us out!'

His little monologue melted the frozen pieces out of my heart, for some time. Then, we had some serious lunch over the city which was rarely impressive in my terms. The food was literally tasty this time around. It was some local 'restaurant' pretty unhygienic but I guess that was why it was succulent.

All throughout the trip I was quite possessive about our meals not about the purity of it but just about the taste and presentation. Where ever I saw a shop I called for brakes, no matter how untidy or pitiful it was. And, I got a fair bit of scolding on such matters in addition my liver had to pay up. It was like a bruise in addition with some salt.

After our meal which took us to the evening we desisted by the hotel, tiredly and skillfully. We sat in to converse on various issues all throughout the night, while we took our momentous dinner and also during the packing scheme for our second last stop.

Back at home, I recalled, I had seen some photos of the temple but those were random show not a thorough look. And, there were obviously of the outer part of the temple not the inner part of it, which urged an emphasizing attitude and made me wonder about its actual design.

However, the little argument that we had in our vehicle made me worried, and I was still working on that part of taking shelter for a night in certainly the coldest part of the country. It was not a fair call for some people while it was a wise one in the eyes of many and certainly it developed a definite hatred in me for the words, "majority" and "democracy"!

I had to convey it to the supreme judge, my mother. 'Look, sweetie it would be fun, we will be in the arms of Lord Almighty, we would have a better chance to stay with him for a whole night, majority of them thrive for this. And, for your uncomfortable part, guess what you can sleep with us (my parents) for that night.' She explained. Well, I had to agree as in these past days or so I haven't been able to sleep with my parents which some time back I didn't prefer to go with. However, I realized that nothing can overshadow the warmth of your parents.

Although, one question sucked into my mind after that debate, 'If we are so fortunate to stay with God for a night, then what can the bunch of people residing in there, be called?'

Anyhow, that little talking comforted me for some time and I knew it was all going to be fine, ultimately.

18

The next morning we were up and into the vehicle pretty quickly and since we had to travel 100 miles it wasn't possible to start trekking KEDARNATH on that day itself so we decided to visit the different sites that would be coming on our way, to the hotel and perhaps get some photos clicked with our memories being saved in our own mechanical hard disk. Possibly, we had to book another hotel but near KEDARNATH city itself, as for, then we could have accurately began our journey early in the morning.

'How many places will be coming in between, some ah worth seeing, ones?' my uncle enquired from the driver. 'Not many sire, but yes some are and they will be worth your while.' The driver said. 'And, that would be?' 'There is this CHAMOLI district, RUDRAPRYAG, DEVPRYAG and UKHIMATH.' The driver answered. 'But, UKHIMATH is almost on the opposite side and will cost us a lot of time thus impugning our schedule, already we are following it with utter discipline.' My uncle sarcastically replied, taking the matchstick out of his mouth with which he was performing experiments in his oral cavity.

'Pull the brakes when we reach CHAMOLI, DEVPRAYAG AND RUDRYAPRAYAG.' My grandfather demanded. I was tangentially confused by the amount of weird names being spoken in front of me. I wasn't even able spell the word correctly and I never could. So, I simply called one of them the "UK PLACE (UKHIMATH)"

However, originally we stopped by to see only, 'CHAMOLI and DEVPRAYAG' for uncertain and dubious reasons which were strictly oblivious to me. We started travelling soon onto that roughly drained road with terminal turns and partly slanting ends. And, just to make things worse we were hit by a long traffic jam. And, adding to our misfortune my uncle started delivering some facts about traffic jam in mountainous region which further scared us. 'These long lanes stoppages are literally the worst in mountainous regions, there is no help provided to you in such hilly areas. Earthquakes are frequent. The traffic jam could be because of a big pathway broken along the lane. If this is so then, I am afraid people, we would have to spend our nights in here, you think of KEDARNATH? We can't even reach our own house; we would be stuck here for days and months to be more specific! But, don't you all worry help will come but only when half of us are either dead of starving or we are about to. And, yet again the helicopters that would be coming to rescue us would fly after taking some, out, that too if you are lucky!'

However, the lane cleared up and we were thankful to God and regretful to ourselves for believing my uncle. All throughout the day, we were either slumbering in our own dreams or gossiping with each other. And, simply for maintaining the conversational flow, I asked, 'What is this UK place all about?' 'UKHIMATH' my brother corrected and laughed on the same instance. 'Whatever! But what is it, anyways?' everyone stared at me, nobody answered.

'Well!' a voice appeared, and it was of my uncle himself, as he continued. 'The place is as sacred as the temple itself. As KEDARNATH is situated at such a height and in the footsteps of Himalayas, it becomes cumbersome for the disciples to get a look at their God in winters, for the place gets covered up by snow and it is difficult to move even an inch, so they shift their God's place from KEDARNATH to UKHIMATH, almost before the festival of light. And the doors open again in April as the snow melts down by inches the number of people visiting increases in thousands. There will be 20,000 people staying up there! For concluding, UKHIMATH is a mini KEDARNATH.' The debate was never ending soon it turned onto, 'PANDITS'-The priest of a temple; And, how abundantly they are found in there and specially in KEDARNATH, further more how much expense they charged for an advance "Look out" in the temple which was defying the line and then looking up to the God. 'So, if you would give them a handsome amount of bucks they will surely deliver you a preferable treatment. Say for instance you give them thousand bucks and the other gives them eleven thousand bucks then the later one would be given a preferable treatment. As, accurate as that!' my uncle explained.

Also, if someone was free enough to stand in a long lane for, "The Look out" then he would get it for free. And, the limit of the payment had no bounds it started with a certain amount and ended with your love and faith towards GOD! 551rs- your Godly faith and huge heart, was the range.

The topic of discussion molded a handful of times, from the weather conditions we straight away jumped onto the skills of our driver. 'It is really unambiguous to defy the skills of our driver, the road is hostile and to drive on such paths that too safely is commendable!' my father said as then my uncle took over, 'On every little turn there are wheels of uncertainty, have a look at the paths; on one side there is a big mountain cut and on the other a deep valley with no railings to protect. And, it is not harsh to drive but actually it is the time duration of his driving and the weather conditions. It is in actual terms a tireless yet watchful job to execute. The cold which gets stuck in their hands while moving the steering which they constantly have to do is quite unbearable on its own. And, then the salary they get is infrequently low, which again is a sympathetical issue to ponder.'

With sleep in our minds and chattering in our hearts we reached onto this village CHAMOLI which was charismatic and contenting in its own way. Although, we didn't stop for long as we had to catch the watch which was leaning ahead of us and so soon we ate our lunch in a local stall and got our irregularly unstable diet. When we used to get into the car I never forgot to carry a bag full of refreshments which were as per my opinion, expired and so was their effect -intense fluid pressure and elevation resulting in nausea and heavy vomiting, as would have been diagnosed by the major population of doctors.

19

It was almost dusk then, and we arrived at this inspiring and blessed place named, DEVPRAYAG. We ceased our vehicle to capture a look at this gorgeous site.

We went down to confine the piece in our souls and it turned out to be a core igniting experience. DEVPRAYAG is basically a place where two rivers, ALAKNANDA and BHAGIRATHI merge into the holy GANGES.

The scenario of two utterly different rivers combining with their beautiful little colors and forming a whole new source with entirely separated color, turned things holy. "By mere imagination, the place can leave you personified while the real encounter with it was far beyond words."

After, DEVPRAYAG we turned our fronts towards GAURI KUND – the place where we were going to stop before reaching KEDARNATH, and was also known as the origin of KEDARNATH. The driver was instructed to speed the vehicle, carefully, for it was crucial to reach a couple of hours before midnight. As, we would then get a suitable hotel to lay our heads down however, there were some contrast in the opinions of the male and the female sides. The males point was to drive it real quick while the females were quite precautious, they asked him to drive with a sudden stability so that we can reach on our residence, safe handedly.

Their debate lasted until we arrived at our destination however in between we saw a big forest fire on our way although we had to get it out of our nerves for there was no time and soon we landed on our be talked place, GAURI KUND or few meters away from it.

As fast as we could have kept our luggage down and would have advised the driver to park the vehicle somewhere, we found a man jogging at us and suggesting us to stay at his hotel. Soon, we discovered that similar to him lots of men were coming towards us as if we were the new and shining 1st grader, again.

After, excusing a majority of them we found our man of the night, he guided us towards his place but before that he threw the facts about his hotel and the most crucial of them was its "budget". He asked us a viable amount of bucks which made us hear him on the first instance, also his hotel was just adjacent to the GAURI KUND so we made up our senses to stay in his hotel.

On the other hand, we advised our driver to come over with us though he turned our offer down as he preferred to stay in there for the night and the upcoming day. Thus, ending his part and who knew that we were seeing him the last time?

The "hotel guy" made us move through those constrained gullies which took us to his place; it was just the kind of place which we were roaming for, it fantasized my genre of hotels.

The name of it was, "SHIVLOK" and I didn't know the meaning of it, though; it was virtually adjacent to the GAURI KUND which was a place where hot water ran exactly 24 hours from a specific top, kind of hot tank which had its own insurance and maintaining society who unsoiled it at a particular time of a day. Also, it had some religious importance of its own!

But, SHIVLOK- the hotel, had been sufficed with its lower part occupied by a restaurant again which could have been accurately identified by being blindfolded due the virtue of the essence sensed walking upward of "THE GREAT INDIAN CURRY" and the upper part consisted of obviously, rooms.

The odor of various food items mainly north and south Indian uplifted my nostrils leading to the formation of saliva and the rooms when seen looked proficient too. Rather, for better, it was superlatively perfect compared to the others. Well kept, maintained and also it had a television set with a good amount of channels which was more than competent for me.

I dived onto the fluffy bed for examining the springs via the air mattress, which obviously didn't make any sense, soon I found it comforting and I grabbed the remote simply to switch on my beloved but suddenly a voice crackled and my hands got frozen on the remote itself, endowing a premonitory shift into the back of my spine. The voice was of my mother argufying with the guy who brought us here, he had turned ironical then, as, he twisted all heads up to betray us and his offer.

He amplified the charge threefold from the initial charge that molded us sometime back. We protested against him by criticizing his ironical demeanor for he got us seductive by some other rate and altered the rate without even confirming us and it wasn't justified.

For a moment we thought of leaving the ground there itself firstly, we had a lot of places to stay secondly, well there was no second thought it was simply his betrayal that had caused this denial.

However, the case was actually a bit different, as we pondered we came to know the big punch on our budget which we would have got for leaving the hotel, it was already overtime, we could have got lost and ¾th of the rooms would have already been booked till then and the rest of them would have charged at an expensive rate almost higher than that one, and if we would have returned back in there accepting to pay the amount in regret we wouldn't have got the room even if we desired to give his demanded money. So, it was quite smart to stay and bargain, as much as we could!

We determined to try one last time although the ladies were given an opportunity to express themselves or bargain for they had this remarkable talent; my mother became the in charge.

We were all wondering that on whose side the matter would go, either the old and greedy guy or my young and ready to bargain mother? Keeping this and some more questions in mind we saw my mother entering into the room.

She expressed herself quite wonderfully in the most sadist of times, for she was expressional less and on the very exact moment I thought that we had lost this superlative building but when she was enquired she said, 'Oh well! He didn't agree on the initial amount.' We all went blank I cursed my luck for this one and not only me each of us got disappointed. 'Hey! Don't be so dull, I said he didn't agree on the initial sum but also he didn't agree on the increased sum, as well.' It was pretty difficult for us to ingest. 'What? Clear the plot, mom!' I demanded.

'Well, just in conclusion we are staying in this hotel, don't you worry, you all can rest now.' My mother answered. The sudden euphoric expressions of my facade could have been abstrusely noticed. Though, the curiosity kept rolling my back.

'How did you pull this one off?' my dad enquired. 'Well, I simply gave some commission to the hotel guy, he wasn't the manager after all and he agreed, and you all owe me one' she said. At last, we had to commend her marketing skills for she concluded, 'That's the way an Indian woman rolls it!'

"Mothers are in real terms the undefeatable aspect of nature!"

20

We got our desired hotel and we sat in to decide upon things which would be aiding us the next day. The majorly discussed topic was, 'Who will go by feet and who on the fatal ponies or by any other suitable means?'

The adultery competition made all the elders cover the distance by walking up to the temple except my uncle who was indolent enough to walk even half a mile and my Grandfather with my two brothers opted for a pony. They said, 'All the kids and the old people with your uncle will go and return on a pony.' And, I was like, 'Am I considered a child over here?'

When I asked my parents about the conspiracy they forced me to get myself back up on the ride, once again. First of all, I never liked riding on a horse shaped animal for instance, a pony after my earlier experience. Secondly, I didn't like the company of my brothers including my lazy uncle. So, that made me an introvert but then it was a compulsion that had to be denied. Also, lastly who would want to miss such an opportunity to reach the holiest of place on earth by any other means other than your legs even if they are medically fit?

Thereby, I had to walk on my feet and I wasn't ready to spend even a single minute without my parents so, A whole walkway without them?

I didn't agree to their deal which was one sided, so I pressurized them a lot by adopting various tactics however they didn't even tremble. For then I adopted and executed one of my well prepared weapon as I said, 'Either I am going on my feet or I am not leaving this hotel.' I desperately demanded my own freedom, but it didn't go quite well on the first place although after much silence and desperate behavior they had to bend down. 'But, what did that make me? Did that molding of a parent against the will of his son made them weak?' some philosophers would have asked.

After a while, we took our dinner from the restaurant downstairs which didn't serve my expectations up to its level, the odor didn't match with the taste in conclusion. After taking our dinner, my father and I went on shopping for some crucial items.

We rented an oxygen cylinder which was of 720 bucks for it would refund us 600 back, the deal was that we didn't have to even open the seal. Also, we bought some latterly used refreshments which were quite expensive than the original amount of the product, although, it became inevitable for us to pick the pieces on the desired rate.

When we got ourselves back to the hotel we found the male members of my family swimming around in a natural hot tub, spanking water like anything. My father and I too went up to get our towels down so that we could have hoped for the same.

I wasn't inclined on the first go, as for, I had to take my clothes off and then I had to jump right through it however I was driven in by my Grandfather's will at that age. He leaped himself into the water which stimulated my blood count as well and so I dived into it.

The sixteen year old boy who was not willing to spend even a second in the hot water spring, wanted to remain in it for his entire social life. Though, I was taken out with a bang by none other than the one who got me in, my father. He feared that the water contained a solid quantity of Sulphur in it which would have lead to uneasiness, vomiting and fainting; as he did in YAMNOTRI. Though, at last when he experienced the same he never came out of it for about an hour or two and he finally concluded that it was a natural spring and it had no Sulphur in it!

However, during my 15-20 minute of swimming for such matter I didn't know how to even move my leg in the water, I simply mimicked some kids who were repeatedly performing the arm action, skillfully. But, the water was virtually magical it got us on our limbs and took all our travelling exertion away in addition it made us lively for the next day.

While, leaving we looked at it for one last time, that night. I had a keen desire to jump in it right through but the water had to be cleaned, so they got us all out while the lady gang were still busy sprawling.

After returning to my room I laid my head down and started watching some random show for only that particular channel was feasible at that particular moment and I didn't know how to operate the box and the mechanism of it was quite an abrupt one for me.

At last, I made up my mind to get my head down under a pillow and sleep until I could as the next day was a huge day on the religious front. We were going to bend our heads down in one of the greatest and ancient INDIAN temple of all and we hoped that complimentary to it would come a memorable and faithful trip!

But, who knew that it was the last decent night sleep of my life?

21

My father woke me up in haste and I saw people running around like anything, getting all dressed up and preparing themselves for that day's occasion.

My father suggested me to take a good bath and freshen myself up as we were then going to depart for the temple. However, I slipped back again to complete my sleep as soon as he turned his head towards the other side. And, I recalled that the previous night I slept pretty late and I couldn't even reach the clinically approved hours of sleep.

Though, he saw me, again and this time he made me stand up on my feet so that I could drive away the dizziness prevalent all around me. But, then again I sat near the window to gain some more rest although I observed that it was still dark.

When I checked on the clock it was still 4 o' clock which intrigued me to ask some data based questions to my father while my saliva was still bobbling in my mouth.

He came near me and briskly commanded me to get myself fresh first, and I had to follow it immediately with no whys and how in my mind.

I soon finished up with my routine and went in the room for taking some more rest but then I cited my father packing up our bags and picking the items that we had planned on the last night. I got him this time for I gripped his hand tightly, and I asked.' Why are we leaving up so early? I mean how can we leave so early, we had other plan, right?' 'We have to leave early, as then we can visit the temple early and we can quickly come back without staying in that cold.' My father said.

I reckoned some aspects about it for a second and it seemed to me that things were now starting to fall in my favor, however, I asked, 'But, why?' 'Well, yesterday night we realized that it was pretty child in here and it wasn't liable to sleep in such cold. And, if this is the condition here, then what will happen to us over there? We will expose ourselves to the thing which we always wanted to avoid, medical illness.' My father answered.

It got me going I knew I had won the trunk and the sick business minded driver had lost it, 'This was my ruling day and this will be the best day of my life!' I said to myself but then his voice appeared, 'Well, don't just sit there, get up and run, also make it quick' my father added and I joined the in color marathon.

I got dressed ultimately with my black jacket and light brown jeans on my lower back and laced my shoes with no socks, apparently I didn't like wearing them. And, we all soon assembled in the basement of the hotel for we decided to leave it but we didn't check out as we would come back again that day itself for our apparently stony will. However, it remained a due for us to pay for that night's stay.

Nevertheless, before we all started walking up to the temple we got our other relatives up on ponies, and it bought us about an hour or so to find the tent under which they were found.

I saw an instructional board which contained directions in it which aided us to move forth and not only that it had some facts also about the temple summed up in it, for instance the height at which the temple was situated, the altitude, latitude and the various little pecks. However, my eyes paused at a point which said, 'THERE ARE CONTINUOUS SHOWERS FOUND EVERYDAY UP ON THE TEMPLE' and the emphasis was on the word "everyday".

It stimulated my curiosity and I feared that it won't be a piece of cake to grasp if it would rain while climbing unlike the first place. So, we had to be quite alert while we moved our legs to and fro.

Anyhow, we all waved a hand towards our other relatives which began their journey on the ponies while we graithed our legs in order to cover up the distance.

And, soon we arrived at the initial point where we would begin our path and again there was a board which said, 'WELCOME TO KEDARNATH BUT BE CAREFUL!' and it also had an emphasis on the word "careful".

As, we started our journey towards the holiest temple on the Earth. Our enthusiasm was at its peak while I was still cracked up by the words, "careful" and "everyday".

But, then it all became a myth when I saw another distance board saying, 'KEDARNATH- 14 MILES'

22

We were all set and moving to commence our journey, all we had to do was to go ahead and cross a bridge, it was dark, sun wasn't seen on the first instance and since the previous day it had been raining a lot in KEDARNATH.

So, we had a fair bit of second thoughts which were dragging our footsteps behind and imprinting us to hold ourselves back in the hotel however we had already let our other relatives go by their respective ponies. 'We can't back out now, can we?' my father said.

The moment we were standing across the railing thinking to move an inch back or forth, a voice appeared. 'Why are you people still standing in here? This is Lord Shiva's palace no one can get harmed, have trust in him.' My uncle said.

We all started clearing our minds and gaining faith in the Lord Almighty's place once again my uncle continued, 'Come on, then! Let us take his name and proceed our way through this journey.' As he crossed the bridge which set an example for us to have faith in HIM and get started, also the little speech that he gave us proved out to be a morale booster!

The trivial nervousness was driven away and we were enthused to begin our journey which when we began walking provided us with a spine to roll on.

As, we moved our leg forth we were provided with a thin and drastic wooden stick which had a pointed nail or some sort of material at its lower tip apparently seeming as a poet's pen just with an enormous size.

However, those were simply similar to the ones used in the FIRST DHAM, where mine got crashed with its nip driven out where else my father's stick broke completely, somehow; unless that was important to mention, although, those sticks were just suitably uncomforting.

The initial mile was slippery which was obviously creamed with, "the routine delivery of the ponies". We adjusted our way through the fragrance of those dead and decayed gram as that was given to them, for I supposed, as their staple diet.

However, it made one thing precise that no matter what genre of an animal you are for instance a Human or animal (though, both are same) grams will always give you gas, even if the amount of consumption remains hideous.

And we had to bear, however my saga cited father later pumped us by his words which stated, 'Do not stop until you have to pee or if you have to maintain your alimentary canal!' virtually in either of the cases all we could do was to get all our secretions back into our respective organs especially the unnecessary ones.

It wasn't even a mile that I had covered then and I already started pulling up deep breaths, exercising my alveolar cavity, sitting on shattered stalls and taking rest.

'Something wasn't right, something was wrong!' my instincts mocked. I had this same feeling when I was on the bus but to make it more worse it was just more imprinting and influential, I had no control over it. It was all a dream on the first instance (on the bus) I couldn't have called shots for then. And, on the bus it was still visible but there while trekking up the temple it was as opaque as a wall. I didn't have any single idea of what was going to happen.

And, then I still regretted if I would have followed that instinct the situation would have been much different! Perhaps, if I had gone to my parents about the matter they would have diagnosed me on the basis of exertion, insomnia or food poisoning, and ultimately I would have ended up on those obscene ponies for the rest of my journey, which I strongly neglected on the first place.

So, it was the best to keep the hole in my mouth shut and focus on self recovery which turned out to be a self diagnosed regret and misery!

"Dark it was, Dark were becoming my senses, Dark had it proved out and Dark had been dominating my thoughts all the way. Sun? There was no sun that day, and neither did we care about it! Nature had sent its most literal metaphors."

"For we were no poets, travelers we were and as travelers we went away!"

23

We paused in for some moments, after we were done walking 2 miles and my head was still burning, there was this unwilling stimuli that made me hide it from my parents.

Walking becomes a burdensome task when you are not willing enough to do so or especially when you have something kept in your stomach so stony that it makes your back propel until you don't hit your nose on the floor regardless if it's a fetus or an over grazed stomach filled with either junk or a strong secret! In addition, when you have to ramble one of the highest and dangerous mountain peaks of the world things just get worse.

However, if you are doing it for a good cause then your posture ultimately begins to balance up and merely that force drives you toward your destiny!

Those were certainly the worst three miles I would have ever walked and especially in that particular journey. Although, it did teach me a lot but it costed me my courage and determination which returned only when I saw a light, not the light of a huge celestial body but a light which had enlightened my nerves or for more which had enlightened my senses.

The sun itself was concealing somewhere near the Horizon above the sky and beneath the clouds! Soon, I saw people walking, running, jogging as fast as they could with no stoppages and in such conditions; it intrigued me and filled the motivating gas into my system which left me walking.

The family members were on top of their feet during the first three miles but as we covered two more miles their blood got cold and their shoulders fell onto their feet, they were exerted, red faced similar to that of a local monkey and worn out like a marathon runner.

The condition of my uncle got severe, his face went blue and voice crackled up like a fourteen year old. Where else, I was moving more prominently than ever! I was uncomfortably comfortable in my own taste.

With a slow rate, ponies started crowding up however the helicopters were still not on the look, the clouds were clear but not for long as we went ahead it grew grayer and clouds gathered around a mountain which seemed as if they were about to land on it!

The grey black clouds had captured the atmosphere like a parasite with sun as its hostage, with it they demanded freedom or else they would have fired their entire bullets in the form of rain! It terrorized each and every little thing to halt but they never did!

"Walking and walking no stopping" the only banner we could hear when we were only a mile away from covering half a distance and reaching to this place known as RAMBADA- it was a stop situated at exactly seven miles from the origin and it indicated that we were half way through the journey and we still had to cover seven more miles. However, we were still a mile away from the half way.

'RAMBADA has developed a lot now! From what I have heard.' a strange person with a grey black moustache seeming like an elderly person although climbing like a young one spoke. We picked up various characters throughout our walk, we started conversing with them, knowing about their lives and telling something about ours for it kept us engaged in our own material and aided us to endeavor our concentration in exertion and made us stride more moderately.

So, this elderly young guy had his own story, he came from GUJRAT and had visited the temple sometime back. Obviously, he was amazed by the extent of variations seen that day from his previous visit to the temple. And, he was sharing his experience with people walking nearby and we were just fortunate enough to walk under his dynasty.

But, for then he was telling some of his own made facts about RAMBADA to us. 'It was nothing absolutely nothing! When I was here in this town before, there were only a few rocks and perhaps some stones to lay your hips down and what some stalls sitting adjacent to it however with no customers all the rights were reserved with us the rates were fixed accordingly and not more than fifty people pausing and taking a break. They didn't even have these distance booth, we just used to start moving our leg and if we see a huge dome shaped heritage we used to consider it as fourteen mile that's it. And, there was no stall in the way not at all just some near the temple that too handful of them.' He said with his loud voice making people aware of the situation.

An old BRAHAMAN who was incessantly listening to his words intervened in between, 'But, now! See those big hotels and DHARAMSHALAS, such big stalls, tents, clinics and what not! It is a city of its own. All the business minded people have thrashed the mountains and have made their respective profitable houses. It is a big spit in the name of the religion! This money generating generation has turned out to be a pinnacle! This divine place of Lord Shiva has been converted into some remains of a market, look at that crowd and look at that mob! I had gone up there me and my wife (pointing towards her) we went up to see HIM, to feel HIM. We have no one in this world, except for each other; we thought that it was a place to open up our nerves, it was a place to get all our solutions but the atmosphere near the temple had fierce reign all around it, it's a whole sale market with people buzzing around everywhere. I have been going to the temple since some time and the numbers of stalls are doubled, hotels have tripled and five times the people! They cut this mountain to make this (pointing downwards) path way wider, but then there is no place for the river to flow in. Someday, it will come up from there (pointing towards the river) to here (pointing towards the pathway).'

We were intrigued by the little monologue of his however we had almost covered half way then and my severe uncle had virtually lost his nerve that time and his condition was getting worse during the span.

Thereby, the females stopped by to check him while my father and I who were walking in the shadow of those knowledgeable men had to leave the conversation there itself. We headed towards our fellow; it was pretty unequivocal for us to leave the ground immediately although soon it became a compulsion.

On the first check we bethought it as a normal stoppage and I considered that we would catch up the conversation, ultimately. However we never could meet them again, they had disappeared into the blues!

As for my uncle he was breathing, deeply, so we thought of it as a routine respiratory issue which was accompanied by severe nausea. Although, soon it malfunctioned us, and so we had to find a remedy for it as we determined to let him cover the rest of his journey by some pony although he was reluctant cause of his self esteem, he didn't desire for quitting when almost half of his distance was covered.

Though, through the persuasive tactics of my aunts about the health related issues he had to give up which then made him cover the rest of his journey to the temple by the means of a bisexual horse, a pony.

As soon as we got him on his little ride we celebrated our independent atmosphere with no unfit personality trekking with us over the enormous hill and we could take care of ourselves and cuddle all the hurdles on our own. "Only the fittest of all were left for survival!"

However, how long could we keep up? How long could we survive more?

24

The scenario after RAMBADA was a bit gratifying; the weather was pleasing for a précised reign while for my first 2 miles I was jogging to digest my beverages that we had ingested during our stoppage over the half way. All my family members were scattered then, just like the first place; some had gone away while some were still mimicking a tortoise.

My aunt wasn't one of them, her tale was that both her husband and son had practically arrived at the temple, where else, she got stuck with us- my father, mother, my other aunt and I!

Therefore, she made it well running in her conscious to cross everyone and arrive at the temple herself so that she could spend some quality religious time with her family (the nuclear one).

Whereby, my father was acting as a guardian for the other two ladies following him while I was leading the trail and moving my limbs as well as I could for the first three miles after RAMBADA. For, I desired to repeat my strategy that I had adopted in YAMNOTRI which was, "Just lead along until someone catches you up!" Ironically no one even smelled me from a distance and so I decided to give up the lead and go back all the way to my parents as I assumed that they would have been worried about me and also I was seized by a thought that what if somehow I was not able to find them? Then I would be chained here forever! With no money to even go back, I was threatened merely by the fact that I would have to work like the laborers for at least half of my living span.

So, I paused for some seconds and then went downwards to look for them and going downwards was not that much wimpy as some would say, the slope was pretty deep and it required control and proper ceasing at précised moments.

After long hours of exploring, I ultimately got my front towards them for they were striving hard and moving their joints as moderately as possible. Also, I could visually capture my father's bored expressions during his walkway with the ladies as a guardian.

Therefore, as a hear some and an obedient kid I went toward him and took his boredom away by confabulating with him, which gave him an inch release from the restlessness. We planned for later happenings in our journey, 'How we would plan the next few hours?' and about the beauty of the place.

However, instantly I remembered something and immediately I confronted my doubt against him which was the story or history of the place which we were trekking, KEDARNATH. I had to enlighten my curiosity up till then. And, so he began narrating the tale as for he had nothing to do better, 'It's an old story perhaps from the time of "Mahabharata". It's a tale about PANDVAS and Lord Shiva. PANDVAS had always been a keen disciple of Lord Shiva but they never could prove that to the God himself. So, they wanted to show themselves and they wished to impress the God, as well. They went to all the possible places where they could have even found his odor which included the KAILASH Mountain. However, Lord Shiva was quite a God in himself and was mischievous too! He had this glimpse in his conscious about the PANDVAS and how they were coming to impress him in his own grounds. And, he as a God had some unearthly powers in him for he transformed himself into a cow and sat near a place which is now known as KEDARNATH. When the PANDVAS came looking for him all they could feel and sense was a cow and snowy mountains. Hopeless and thwarted they turned their back to check for him in some other place although "BHEEM" the strongest of the five brothers found it quite strange that only a cow was sitting alone with no organism nearby. He got suspicious and soon he started moving close to the cow. Lord Shiva considered that BHEEM had discovered his little secret so the cow (Lord Shiva) started digging the ground such that he could escape from there. But, before he could complete his exeunt BHEEM had already gripped his back and tail. He applied all of his force to pull him back up, while the others we still forming notions about it; where else BHEEM had almost taken the cow out of that hole and he turned back while holding him (Lord Shiva) to inform the other four brothers about Lord Shiva sneaking away like this. Instantly, the cow slipped back from his hands and before he could have mulched and grasped him back again the upper or the former part had already taken its resignation letter. His front portion had escaped completely however the lower part of the cow remained in the hands of the powerful guy leaving his tail and the 2 pairs of leg suspended over the ground which resembled Lord Shiva. Thereafter, out of their keen devotion towards the God they established this temple and the lower part of the cow as its symbol; years after it came to be known as KEDARNATH!'

The myth was pretty mesmerizing, combining both logic and belief. All of them had a unique place in my heart but that one engulfed a sense of devotion in like no other story or myth could! But who knew, that after some hours all of it was going to be turned into a myth, as well!

25

Twelve miles were covered then, with utter determination and devotion especially in those last few. Though, after that it became rigid both the surface and our will, plus already we were walking quite drastically. My dad had cramped his leg a couple of times before due to the extreme cold conditions. It wasn't whelming for me to see to my father suffering with that cramped leg, but all we could do was just to apply some spray or perform certain physical medication.

And, it certainly did aid him as his first on. All of us felt a falling force pushing us to dive across the valley while the pain was at its epitome and our bodies were simply hanging with no internal energy or soul!

Then, all of a sudden I felt a few rays of light massaging my cells mushily and moderately as they were! For, the light of a huge mass body, it was! And, simultaneously it delivered us our lively souls back into our worthless bodies.

For a moment we thought that it was a moral aspect of our journey, for a moment we thought that this magnificent conception of God has spread its wings all over us. It had enlightened us to walk through the doors of Heaven! But was that all it? Obviously no! Or, was it just something good playing its part, for something worse was about to enter the stage?

"Slowly did we go and slowly did we proceed!" those few moments had made us more resolute towards our destiny and keen towards revising our own pain.

Gazing at every board which indicated the distance to Heaven! One mile then progressively half a mile and then it was some meters away, as the measuring scale changed by a perplexing margin.

Every single earthly person would have in their entire life tried to imagine the HEAVEN but no one would have dreamt of the outer environment surrounding the heaven. Well, it was grey, dark and wet. It was consistently raining from the previous night although when we went near the premises the rain had desisted and the weather out was at its best as compared to some previous rainy nights.

Some yards away yet miles far were we as went near and adjacent to the tropically designed atmosphere in the Indian subcontinent. Just after covering four miles from the origin the top of the temple was partially seen and it attained its virtual visibility when we were meters away from the sight. The uppermost dome of it glazed with a brighter contrast like that of a star, reflected along the cloudy and hilly surface.

However, the entire model of the temple was pretty clear as we were all about to enter the premises. We could walk, then; through the wet surfaces, we could smell then, we could feel then. God was near! God was rather some steps away!

The oxygen level was low but the fragrance of that positive atmosphere was capable enough to let us grow old in there, it was more than efficient. And, one could define happiness in accurate terms in there which ultimately according to me was none definable, which said that, "Happiness had no define but purity, ethics and morality, did."

On the same instance we were full of emotions, now that we have reached our destination, now that, I was standing in front of HEAVEN!

We got near the temple, but before letting our feet enter in and having bend our heads down against the God or simply feeling his mere presence we felt a need to find our other family members as they were waiting for us from a good duration!

And, there they were! Sitting all around forming an imperfect sphere. 'Hey! Enjoyed your rides, eh?' my father asked. 'Yes, we did! And, we went in too it was quite something, go on in quickly before it starts to rain again.' said my health conscious uncle with an amusing sigh.

We handed our material including our footwear to them and started walking towards ECSTASY!

26

My father asked me and my mother to go and buy a plate of the, "Donating materials" which were going to be submitted to the priest who would present it to Lord Shiva by placing it in front of his sculpture for some time but just for some time as there would be others in the line too and Lord Shiva would have to eat theirs, as well.

Although, my aunt too decided to go with us and acquire some for her family (the nuclear one) as well. Where else my other aunt had already gone in two times due to her obscuring nature and opportunist tendency. So, only I, mother, my father and my aunt were left but they decided to let me go with my aunt as my parents were going together on a special pass consisting of some crap loads and it was determined after we had taken our plates full of stuffs.

However, until that my mother and I were all alone, excluding my nature loving aunt who was busy gazing at the wonderfully wet site. My mother started adoring the beautiful aspect of the temple and the Himalayas but suddenly she turned towards me; she glanced at me for certain unrealistic seconds; the proud eyes had said it all, though, she tried to express her feeling within words but they weren't sufficient and also the fact that I don't clearly remember her words.

Though, she was proud and well aware of the fact that I was gritty enough to cover the entire distance on my feet while the rest of the kids couldn't even think of it. "The best feeling in this entire universe is to make your mother proud of your existence!" I quoted to myself.

Perhaps, even I couldn't believe for once that I had attained such a distance but then after staring at that magnificent architecture I could proudly be an optimist.

We purchased all the necessary items in the plate which was ethically decorated, for it costed as much as a Smartphone. And, we got back to my father who had two passes in his hand and it enthralled my living behavior; I was jumping around to take hold of it and complete my inner tour of the temple as briskly as possible for I was well exerted. But, I had to give up my desire as my parents considered it necessary to go as a privileged couple; the ticket was meant for an elderly young single child couple who left me with my aunt and we had crossed our way through the Indian crowd.

We two were quite satisfied as we were going through the normal lane than by hiring some religious broker in for our entrance. The line was gigantic and massive which made me a bit sick (mentally). There were various people along that line some waiting to reach into the temple, some perhaps chattering with people and the others started worshiping Lord Shiva. However, an exception was found in the midst of that huge line of all believers and devout- An Atheist!

He stood behind my back and stupefied all the rituals and pointless practices which were of no logic and an immaterial principal which came into existence by an unknowing presence in addition he wanted everyone to be in his category, an Atheist. 'There is no God! All of this is entirely rubbish! Have you ever seen him? Felt him? Got up to his palace? You think you are his disciples by singing his songs, by calling his name every time when you are in trouble and you think he will help you but no he won't! Did he? When I was standing up that night praying for my wife and children's safety; where was he then? Where were his miracles! I want you people to open your eyes and conclude it yourself that the word, 'God' is nonexistent! You must be wondering that why this old man has come here that why this old man is cursing your only hope? But, there isn't one! Couple of years ago me, my wife and my kids were leaving for YAMNOTRI we had our God's photograph in our car and there was this another car speeding up; it was night and they were drunk! I wanted to save them and I lost control; the car fell into the valley. With me left alone! Left with my solitude and THE REMAINS OF MY FAMILY! I prayed, I cried and I begged for life! Not for me but for my family and I wished death for me! He didn't give me anything rather he took away everything. He is not there and you all are Fools!' he said.

I had to change his perceptions; there was no chance he was walking off like that by his one side conversation. 'How come can you call yourself an Atheist? Atheist are people who don't have any faith in any commodity either the negative or the positive but I guess you have because such confidence and trust on God being not there does prove that you have faith. So, you aren't an atheist that's one point. You are the biggest believer sir you should know that; you lost your children and your wife in a car accident which triggered you to defy his mere existence? Perhaps, go out and live the agony of other beings; their pain is no less than yours but they don't come here to convert anyone and show hatred against, well, someone you don't even believe into. It seems to me as if you were a disciple of him yourself; you believed; you loved but now that you're faith is broken you are just confused of where to go and whom to cry with. I shall tell you one thing sir you are and you will always be a believer no matter what happens after that. Let it out, sir; Let it out! Cry! Don't let them know your hatred but your pain. And, let that force get into you! Then, stand up and go back to what you used to do! Live it till you have it. And, sir — Just believe!'

That is exactly what I wanted to advice him but sadly I couldn't. I was a 16 year old kid, they said. What would I know?

27

S oon, it began to rain and I felt unsafe and frustrated, I never did like any cold and wet thing on either my head or on any part of my body, but there I was getting all wet.

Then, I had this translucent thought which didn't allow me to enter the temple rather it made me get out of the line to my parents who had then already finished their bit; also it could have been because of that old man but well, who cared.

They assumed that I had been in the temple however they inquired from me about my aunt, the thing was that my aunt forgot my presence in the midst of that line so she worked her way through the crowd and went inside the temple thus leaving me all alone and I couldn't notice it, somehow; I was well mingled with the old man's dilemma. And, it proved out be one of the reasons of my walk out!

So, when my parents inquired from me about her, I lied to them; I told them that I found an opening in the middle of the crowd lane early on, but it was simply not enough to fill it for a 16 year old boy; I too adjusted with great difficulties so there was no chance for my aunt to enter into that spot. Thereby, my aunt went backwards to go for the look out as she couldn't find any place for herself. And, when my aunt came rattling out of the temple I told her the other way round, which was enough for her to consume it as a raw material, for she didn't care.

However, I regretted this assessment of mine; I cursed myself for not going inside the temple. After all that effort, I didn't go in; I couldn't even sense HIS presence. It was all a myth for me, then. Although, later I was given a rebirth, as were going to break once again the next morning for the weather was getting bad and my family members advised and decided as a whole to rent a Hotel until the next morning and determined to opt for plan B which we had agreed to the driver.

The hotel was rather an introvert in itself, to say the least! The walls had cracks gifted as a legacy to it; the ceiling was leaking; the bed sheets had huge holes in it, dust was a common observation and the blankets which would protect our body from the adverse cold themselves needed some shelter!

Although, we were actually waiting for the rain to break so that we could have bought some food for the entire family (the joint one). As for, we didn't take our breakfasts before our departure.

The weather had some different plans for us; it was raining since the previous night and things were shaping out be a bizarre. We all had picked up our rooms though only two of them were available, and after settling our materials over the line I went towards my father as he was standing adjacent to the door and was gazing towards the long and flat drop delivered from the sky. "Sometimes the love towards the other being increases just by staring at them, you realize how adorable they are and what's their place in your life." And, I knew one thing that I certainly loved him a lot! But, that day was a mere gift of realization off course.

I walked up to him and stood by his side just as a perfect woe of a couple would. In utter silence and melancholy I was staring at him while he continued looking outside the corner. I gently placed my unabashed neck on his shoulder to let him sense my presence and in response he turned his head lucidly toward me and passed a lighthearted smile at me.

I knew that he was pride about my succession, also, I knew that it wasn't a great achievement to trek a mountain of fourteen miles long with random services and facilities provided into your hands. But, still my achievement was actually a relevant one, none of my brothers could have hiked so far, but I did amongst them which according to the Indian set of parents were a hefty establishment. However, he felt it best to express his emotions with his style, a gentle smile.

And, so we both stood slantingly and gazed at the wonderful aspect of nature!

28

'This is the worst rainfall ever! The thunder is tremendous; I have never seen such a rain happening in Kedarnath, at this time of the year.' A voice came, probably from the manager's table, as for, the manager was talking to some random guy.

We interrupted our natural scenario and went near him. 'So, what do you think is the condition? Will it stop?' my dad inquired. 'I don't know sir, but, it doesn't seem like so; this is the worst rainfall which I have encountered in my 20 years of career.' the manager answered his bit.

'It doesn't look good to me!' my father said horrendously. And, we went in the room to warn our other family members about the unsung disaster. 'Nature is planning a trip of its own, things won't be comfortable now, this place isn't safe anymore; Kedarnath isn't safe, anymore!' my father warned my family members.

We weren't safe I knew that but up until then some merely preferred to call it an abnormal shower. Although, I wasn't surprised at all, I knew it would rain, as per the instructions mentioned in the initial entrance board.

However, it never stopped raining and in the middle of that we had to take our food while the clouds were replacing each other contentedly, as for, evening it was going to be.

Also, we had our meal as some crispy Pakoras and some native dish which set in for the imperfect last dinner, of my span!

Rain hadn't cleared up, so we had to procrastinate our plan of leaving that day; and, we had then completely adopted plan B. And, were going to depart in the morning after attending the routine prayer session without any further delays, also, my father promised me to buy me some good breakfast from a three starrer restaurant.

All throughout the evening we debated on diversified topics, as we were excited to leave for our last halt, Badrinath. And, who knew that it was the last conversation with my family and with my parents!

We had taken a plethora of memories with us which could never be shed and we were going to take certain memories which would outlive it all!

We had to sleep a bit earlier that evening considering the lack age of spicy topics and our exertion during the journey. So, we went inside our beds to take a good night sleep and arise fresh the other day!

But, once we had slept in we couldn't arise more!

29

Little bit of nap and that was enough for a last pleasing night; but then still I was trying enough to take my bit of slumber; my parents weren't sleeping with me they were there in the second room that we had rented, ironically. And, I had no alternative other than that for I forgot to get my last sleep with them, insanely and totally.

The thunder was bursting in pieces out there, where else the precipitation from the unfazed clouds was performing its medial role from certain hours, then. And, simultaneously the fast blowing winds were heard while my brother was shivering for the same.

Our entire efforts were to get him one more blanket to rest upon and cover his shoulders and neck certainly but that didn't satisfy his internal heat captivated by another blanket. On obvious basis, he was captured all around by some random virus named, Rhino!

And, same was with my mood! It was anxiously disgusted around the place, also, I couldn't sleep; my conscious was over my preconceived notions of staying in the bed at night. I went off the covering to have a real quick look of the scenario going on outside.

As, I opted to embrace the outer representation it looked pretty normal to me as some place raining and wet would be!

Although, the insect of self suicide would induce some unlikely thoughts in your veins and would let you die by your stupidly sane decision and it proved to be the last one of my span. Just to check further I stirred a bit ahead, outside the hotel near a shelter made of thick and molted iron with some low quality polyester on it.

I had this dubious feeling to step my foot out of the door which smelled like old squelchy grass and chicken as well, and have a check on the inhabited condition prevailing outside.

However, that angle seemed quite normal to me as well, there was no such force which could tear apart my fragmented respect and love for my parents and my family at large. I turned my front back towards the hotel to spend the rest of my night and life with my parents. I imagined a dream in a dream that I would be lying in between my parents as a kid and I would hold them tight not just to avoid the cold but also to show my token of respect and love towards them.

I vowed that I wouldn't make them unhappy for any such cause also I promised myself that the next time I visit this Heaven named KEDARNATH, I would take them on my shoulders as then they wouldn't be able to make it till here by themselves and if it wasn't possible then I would bring them up by helicopters, when I would publish bucks, as a clerk. Or perhaps saving someone or most probably writing but that depended on the phase off course.

But, all of a sudden a vibrant wave came down my throat but not as massive as it was in the atmosphere for an earthquake it was! And, quite a huge one!

Everything and anything present around the premises started shivering and vibrating not as some smart phone would although thousand times more than it and quite briskly too! Every accessible particle had frozen onto its mean position while they were vibrating with a sudden motion in the midst of its own effervescence. Like the earth's rotation had increased fourfold, instantly; like the two poles were going to exchange their places; like the dead bodies submerged in were pushing the ground to arise from being dead and bring on a new part of life, death!

And, I was down, kneeling on the floor as no body and with no assurance of the next moment and ironically, I felt something being dropped on my head which almost took my parietal lobe away.

I was leaning on the floor with some red fluid and my forebrain thrashed all around the place by none other than that shelter which was standing right up to me before I could catch hold of anything it was onto me, and I went to some other world!

30

'**H**ush! Hush! Looks as if he is alive.' Someone whispered. I somehow tried to open my eyelets which were pretty swollen to look at some disgusting creatures with mud covered face starring at me as if I had taken their private organs for rent.

They woke me up, made me sit and I tried to recall my last known and virtual happening, for, I tried to move my neck at an angle of 180 degree. And, the differential speed of my first neck movement to the second neck movement had a huge leap in between.

I checked in and around but astonishingly my hotel or the place where I was staying in the previous day had, vanished. I further checked the other scenes and they were too gone, entirely; the stall which was there till the previous day didn't even give a clue of its presence.

The stalls, the footwear shop, the sweets shop, hotels, Dharamshalas, People? My family? All had gone but I wasn't able to digest the later. The mere thought of it gave me some mind bobbling Goosebumps!

I inquired from the other fellow beings about my family; I gave them an idea; their texture, appearance and perhaps everything but no success!

Nothing and nobody could be seen except the temple, some stones and remains all over the ground which was mud and concrete little pebbles, also, with some clothes which had bump over it and after later investigations came out to be a dead body! 'What's that bumpy cloth doing there?' I asked. 'That's a dead body, kid!' he answered.

I didn't know what happened, what was the cause and where was my family? The questions were never ending I had to get my thirst of curiosity satisfied, so I ceased this guy passing adjacent to me who was wandering about like a psychopath, as I was lying over the highly cracked up place. 'What happened sir, help me sir, I was lying here the previous night with all the stuff in front of me and now it's all gone, what happened?' I asked. 'It's all over! This is all over! New world! New beginning! Kalyuga has ended.' He commented and went away in his own tone thus leaving me dazzled.

I couldn't even get his words rightly and precisely he confused me even more. Something had occurred, maybe that earthquake? And, certainly that earthquake! But, where were my family members, where were my parents?

And, if something ill happened then where were the remains? Where was that hotel?

Soon, I understood the man's pain and I too wandered about in search of my family with some serious cut on my head and pre traumatic stress. I had to stand up and look for my family even if it wasn't that feasible for me. And, it was complex to do so; especially, in such rocky terrain filled up with random and gritty cracks which were no longer certain.

I found a person rescuing people and the same face that took the shelter off my worthless body. I adjusted myself first; I sat on the filthy ground adjacent to a person shifting sides on a mattress. 'Excuse me, sir? Can you tell me what caused all this (looking towards the ground)?' I enquired. Although, he was pretty busy in his own work, which was commendable; he ignored my voice and I wasn't willing enough to ask it off, once again. So, I sat with a depressed mood and visage toward the ground.

'Cloud burst! There was a cloud burst and hence this landslide and thence this earthquake in addition to a major flood that took it all away, which took everyone away! It was a multiple bizarre!' the man lying adjacent to me answered while wiping off his tears.

I shifted near him a little; to conquer my hopeless curiosity!

31

The guy was old and pinnacled; one had to speak at louder amplitude in order to make him get your words; for his ears were bleeding, sorely. 'There was this hotel, right there (pointing towards it). I had my family in there, the previous night; Do you have any ah idea that where it might be?' I called in a loud and stammering manner. 'No hotel! Nothing! It all flew away, wake up my friend; IT ALL FLEW AWAY!'

I couldn't get hold of myself; everything was down, it went cold and I lost all my hope for there was no one left!

I was virtually dead for some pale cold seconds. 'But how can the hotel disappear, just like that?' I got up with my anguished heart and asked with a capturing tone. I knew what the answer would be but how couldn't I try more? If there was even a single percent chance left of their come back or any information about them, I would have named all my gems after him.

'You talk about a hotel? The whole city of KEDARNATH is gone, it's it! He replied, rudely. It looted away my residual volume and left me Asthmatic, I fainted twice or thrice during the course.

Sitting along the line to get some diet for my survival which had just a mere name added to it; exhausted and superlatively in tensed with no means of living! "Who shall take care of me? Who would scold me when I'll do a bad thing? Who would buy me a new rIng? Who would enjoy with me? To whom would I share my emotions and donate my motions? To whom would I ask for new gadgets? And, who would be happy if I improve their budget? Whom would understand my living or dead sorrow? Whose agony would I promise to borrow? To whom would I give? And, with whom would I live?" I asked myself.

Though, I determined to walk, certainly as an injured hero would! But, I had to, and I had to get my family; I had to explore them; I had to! And, so I never gave up!

I went to and fro, repeatedly. Simply seeking a clue which would lead me either to my family or eternity; 'What if both eternity and my family are on the same place?' the question arose frequently. And, I lost all the hope but still I never ceased their search.

And, the rescuing process began, with me sitting alongside the wall getting wet but not caring to hide from the odd. Nights passed and so did days, there was no sign of them, my family, and "my parents".

I confirmed my worst nightmare after being exerted of trying hard for days but not because I lost all the hope but due to my impatient nature with my own eyes and mind, yes they were no more; they were dead!

The place had converted into turmoil; from a busy crowded area it turned into a silent and melancholic, graveyard with dead and decayed bodies all around and every time a dead body was taken and burnt away; there itself I started searching my family in them, with a heavy heart. But, yes I did! Just to seek their last look no matter how bad it was; no matter how demeaned it was. I simply wanted to confront my love towards them; I had a lot to say but then it all remained inside!

All the survivors had lost their pals, and yes they did survive but for nothing; nothing to live for! Some lost their mothers, some wives, some sisters, some best friend; some couples lost their partners and me? I lost my entire family. A 16 year old boy, the most unfortunate of the lot yet in the names of those few lucky ones!

The survivors had nothing to live for; some committed suicide by jumping off the valley but some looked for a ray of hope while the others like me which were exposed to suicidal thoughts though didn't murder themselves just because nature had planned a different treat for them!

"They had to wait, wait to thrive, and wait to die while some waited for an absolution that would never come!"

After, looking at each of its bit and pondering about which stall I would be working in to earn my living and forgetting my past; at least trying to I erase the ones which were life taking. I always had this feeling of being happy in every little bit of circumstances that life throws towards you, as, everything happens for good! But no! Not this time. Nothing was good, it was worse accurately. Nothing could be normal again and I had lost my will and desire; it broke my faith in humanity and from God!

32

*S*itting in while bending my knees which touched my forehead stringently, perhaps planning to take a try with suicide as I was! And, that too in the same valley and on the same spot where the hotel collapsed.

And, all throughout the days I calculated my survival for how I survived? There was this enormous flow of water and earthquake that came and the later disaster lead to the collapse of a metallic sheet which was by chance thin and it fell onto me. Fortunately, when the flood came the direction of it was changed due to some inapprehensive reason. It moved onto the other side to take onto the hotel in which I was staying!

That took my family with it and every day I tried to visit that place where that hotel was and I hoped to dive into that valley but I was not that willing. I wanted to live but die!

I reckoned various ifs and buts including my own departure and arrival plus I criticized myself for it; I pondered about the various ways I could have saved them or how I would have joined them by making myself a dead person for better. But, I knew it wouldn't aid; but, yes it did engage me!

However, this time I was sitting beneath this age old mountain protecting my head from the continuous rains. I suddenly heard another piece of voice banging in my ears but it was moderate than the previous one. And, suddenly I sensed my death.........

I stood up to grasp the sound and respond to it, ultimately; so that I could have ran on the opposite side of it, if something was there.

I couldn't see anything coming on the first instance however accordingly I saw my death!

A land slide was coming towards me with a tremendous velocity; I knew there was no escaping it and that was the best opportunity to get my dream fulfilled; all I had to do was just stand and surrender! Though, I felt bad for the others who had to live but there at that place I was given the finest gift of life, death!

So, I stretched my arms for no reason perhaps that was it. My family was calling me, then; Lord Shiva was calling me, and then; Eternity was calling me!

I closed my eyes for one final time in that entire journey and let that death welcome me into her bloody arms!

I was dead on virtual and half literal basis and the memories of the past days where it all began, started rewinding in front of my eyes!

And, so I got a sudden jerk, which took me from that place and got me to HAVEN!

Epilogue

"**P**ast or future, I do not desire anything, all I want is to live; live in my present; live infinitely with the ones I love, now and forever!"

I have never felt so alive before, as if something huge was taken off from my head leaving me free; free from all the strings; free from every little thing that constrained my living emotions, it's as if all my pain and agony were taken within a second and I was left dazzled and puzzled about my future however quite certain about my present!

A sharp white little was captured by my eye yields there was no life after death they said, but I passed on to the phase of eternity and yes life was after death! There was no chance that I could have got into heaven; my Karma balance was not so supportive enough to lead me in there but there was this positive vibe all around me and I definitely knew it was heaven! My education said it was heaven!

Stereotypically, heaven had an entirely white atmosphere however I wasn't able to open my eye balls and how could I? It was no earth, it wasn't natural; I was in God's place; I was in Heaven!

'Heaven will be amazing! I have got the games, got the girls, I have the power but do I need all of that? I don't know, although I will surely need my parents; I have something to tell; I have something to confront and I shall surely deliver them my feelings and I promise I won't be shy!' I said to myself.

Heaven was what life was all about being dead but being immortal at the same time. The urge for probing my parents was more than that of God himself! I needed my family and parents more than I preferred the ultimate power. It was something unusual yet desired!

I wanted to grasp it all; every little hope and desire of mine but I had to make an effort; I had to get up and had to look for my parents explore them and then thrive with them for the rest of my after life; that was forever.

And, so I made an effort I started unbolting my eyes as gently as possible and there was this gist of uncertainty grasped by my senses.

I opened them completely for I wanted to look forward to heaven and I saw some pictures which were quite known to my senses. I stretched my swollen eyelids simply to increase my vision and get the facts right for I found myself in an upper cabinet of a bus going to Haridwar!

But I died and they did too for it was THE IMMORTAL DEATH!

The End